A Practical Guide to Food Law in the United Kingdom

2nd Edition

Ian Thomas is a dual-qualified specialist food lawyer practising in England and Wales (barrister 1993) and in the Republic of Ireland (solicitor 2006).

Ian has substantial experience of advising or appearing in court in relation to a wide range of food law matters including; food safety and hygiene, animal welfare (including at the time of killing), food information, health and nutrition claims, food supplements, borderline products, traceability, product withdrawals and recalls, official controls and enforcement powers.

He works with clients in Ireland, the UK, Europe and from around the world and is able to provide advice to clients on both national (England and Wales and Republic of Ireland) and EU law.

Ian is a Visiting Professor at Ulster University (Faculty of Life and Health Sciences) where he provides lectures and course material for the PgC/PgD/MSc Food Regulatory Affairs and Veterinary Public Health courses.

He is an elected Fellow of the Society of Food Hygiene and Technology, and a member of the Food Law Group and the Food Safety Professionals Association.

Ian is the author of two books published by Law Brief Publishing:

'A Practical Guide to the Law Relating to Food': and

'Covid-19 and the Law Relating to Food in the UK and Republic of Ireland: The Essential Guide'

"Extremely knowledgeable in his field." "He inspires confidence in his clients and is highly skilled at handling all the detail in a case."
– Chambers and Partners

"A true food safety expert, he has a grasp of pitching his in-depth, technical knowledge in the most appropriate commercial context."
– Legal 500

A Practical Guide to Food Law in the United Kingdom
2nd Edition

Ian Thomas
Barrister-at-Law, 6 Pump Court, London
Solicitor, Ian Thomas Associates, Republic of Ireland

Law Brief Publishing

Published 2021 by Law Brief Publishing, an imprint of Law Brief Publishing Ltd
30 The Parks
Minehead
Somerset
TA24 8BT

www.lawbriefpublishing.com

Paperback: 978-1-914608-28-5

For Mary, Aisling, Ciara and Poppy

And for my mom, dad and brother Edward

Thank you for everything

PREFACE

There is a framework of many rules and regulations that ensures, or is intended to ensure, that food is safe, has been produced in hygienic conditions and is as described. This is called food law.

Modern food law can be traced back to a series of food incidents in the 1990s which highlighted that consumer protection needed to be achieved at EU level, rather than being left completely to the individual Member States to organise, regulate and enforce.

The Executive Summary to the European Commission's White Paper on Food Safety published in 2000 stressed the importance of the EU having the highest standards of food safety. In order to achieve this, a radical new approach was proposed.

The basis for this new way of doing things was set out in one of the most important pieces of EU food law; Regulation 178/2002 – the General Food Law Regulation.

The European Food Safety Authority (EFSA) was created to apply a science-based approach to food safety and to prepare advisory scientific opinions on a wide range of topics such as, nutrition, health claims and the safety of individual foods and ingredients (see for example the EFSA Opinion on the safety of titanium dioxide (E 171) in May 2021 which recommended that the substance should no longer be regarded as safe for use as a food additive).

EU food law has developed by enacting more and more regulations which are "binding" and "directly applicable in all Member States" (including the UK prior to 1 January 2021). With some important exceptions, EU food law has therefore become more uniform so that the same law applies in each Member State.

The overall objective of EU food law is a high level of protection of human life and health and the protection of consumers' interests, including fair practices in food trade.

Food that has been made in accordance with applicable laws may be traded freely within the EU.

The United Kingdom of Great Britain and Northern Ireland was a full member of the EU until 11 pm (UK time) on 31 December 2020 (which is referred to in this book as IP completion day). Since then, it is, for the purposes of the EU, a "third country".

Trade between the UK and the EU is no longer free and frictionless and there have been many instances of how these changes have had an adverse impact on both parties and on their citizens. In many respects, trade between Great Britain and Northern Ireland is no longer completely free and frictionless

In general terms, EU food law still plays a fundamental part in the food law of the United Kingdom, although more precisely this should mean the law of Great Britain (GB – England, Wales and Scotland) as EU food law continues to apply in Northern Ireland (NI).

EU food law, in the version that was in force on IP completion day continues to apply, subject to various amendments to make it workable in and applicable to GB. This is part of a new domestic legislative regime called retained EU law.

Although we speak of GB to mean the 3 nations together, it is important to recall that food is a devolved power and that the competent authorities in England, Wales and Scotland are responsible for food policy in their respective jurisdictions.

Thus, we have a situation in which GB and the EU are separate and distinct and, in theory (and sometimes in practice), England, Wales and Scotland are separate and distinct in terms of food law and policy.

In order to mitigate against the potential adverse consequences of food being a devolved power, and to ensure that goods can be traded freely throughout the United Kingdom, the Internal Market Act 2020 came into force on IP completion day.

The departure of the UK from the EU has resulted in many significant changes to GB food law. Although many of these may be seen as matters of form (e.g. substituting the name of GB institutions authorities for the name of EU bodies), they are also very much matters of substance (e.g. those GB authorities are now responsible for authorisations for products to be placed on the GB market).

UK food law, including its application in NI, has changed and the mindset of UK (particularly GB), EU and global food lawyers and advisers. They and food businesses need to adapt to the new legal landscape.

Nevertheless, some aspects of food law have not changed. Food businesses continue to have a duty to ensure the food they make and sell is safe and as described. They will continue to be subject to regulatory scrutiny with non-compliances being actioned and cases will still to go court in much the same way as before.

In this book I shall use the term UK when referring to general matters relating to the UK, the term GB to mean England, Wales and Scotland combined and NI means Northern Ireland.

References to EU Regulations are to the versions applicable in GB as retained EU law (i.e. the version of the Regulation that was in force in the UK on IP completion day).

When referring to domestic legislation, I have tended to quote from the version of regulations applicable in England and then made reference to equivalent regulations applicable in Wales and to Scotland. No discourtesy is intended to readers looking for the Welsh and Scottish legislation.

The NI situation is very fluid and at the time of writing, November 2021, the UK and the EU are discussing the future arrangements for how food will be regulated and traded to and from NI.

It may be useful to explain what this book is not about, as well as what it is about.

There have been many changes in customs law, import and export controls and trade practices and procedures as a result of the UK's departure from the EU. These are specialist areas of law and are not covered in this book other than in passing when relevant to a particular topic or discussion. In a similar vein, this book does not go into detail about the UK's domestic Withdrawal Acts or the Trade and Cooperation Agreement between the UK and the EU.

Time and space have prevented any detailed references to many topics that are relevant to food law; security, sustainability, climate change to name a few.

Unfortunately, for the same reasons, it has not been possible to discuss many important areas of food law (such as organics, novel foods, food improvement agents, foods for specific groups and food contact materials). The areas I have selected are because I believe, rightly or wrongly, that they will be of the broadest appeal to readers.

Above all, this book is intended to be a practical guide to the way food law is now enacted, regulated, and enforced in the UK, or more precisely in GB. It is not, nor is it intended to be a heavyweight legal textbook.

The natural risk of such an approach is that it has not been possible to provide an in-depth approach to some legal issues and some have not been covered at all, or sufficiently to meet every reader's expectation or needs.

This book may be useful for anyone with a professional interest in food law and regulation whether as students, academics, business operators, workers in the food industry or legal and regulatory professionals. It may also be of interest to anyone who wants a general introduction to the way in which UK food law has developed and continues to develop since 1 January 2021.

I would like to thank everyone who has helped, supported and motivated me throughout my career both in the UK and Ireland; family, friends, food professionals (lawyers, scientists, advisers and consultants), colleagues inside and outside the legal profession and, finally, to the barristers, clerks and staff at 6 Pump Court.

I also wish to thank Tim Kevan and Garry Wright of Law Brief Publishing for allowing me the opportunity to write this second edition which I hope is informative and interesting, but above all useful, if only as an aide memoire or as a basic reference point for the busy reader.

Any comments or observations made in the book are personal and do not necessarily reflect the view of others. All errors in the text are mine and mine alone.

Food law an exciting and interesting subject and has without doubt become more complex and challenging. Food law is now a truly a distinct and specialist area of law.

The law in this book is based on legislation in force on 1 November 2021.

Ian Thomas
November 2021

CONTENTS

Chapter One	Food Law in the UK	1
	Introduction	1
	The four nations of the United Kingdom	1
	The UK outside the EU	2
	The free movement of food within the EU	4
	The free movement of food within the UK	5
	Northern Ireland	6
	The continued impact of EU food law in Great Britain	7
	Making food law relevant to and applicable in GB – EU Exit Regulations	9
	EU Exit Regulations – an example	10
	Interpreting food law	13
	Conclusion	14
Chapter Two	The Regulation of Food Businesses and Foodstuffs	15
	Introduction	15
	Registration and approval of food businesses	15
	EFSA – now GB expert committees and appropriate authorities	17
	Products requiring authorisation	18
	Placing a product requiring authorisation on the market in Great Britain	19
	Conclusion	22
Chapter Three	Food Safety	23
	Introduction	23
	Retained EU food law and the 'EU Exit' Regulations	23
	The principles of food safety	25
	Practical application – a case of food poisoning	31
	Conclusion	35

Chapter Four Food Hygiene 37
Introduction 37
Retained EU food law and the 'EU Exit' Regulations 38
A particular change to Regulation 852/2004 in the EU 39
Hygiene of foodstuffs – the general rules – Regulation 852/2004 48
Practical application – enforcement action under the hygiene regulations 51
Conclusion 52

Chapter Five Food Information to Consumers 53
Introduction 53
Retained EU law and 'EU Exit' Regulations 54
Allergens and PPDS – a recent UK development 54
The Provision of Food Information to Consumers Regulation 1169/2011 (FIC) 55
Responsibilities for food information – Article 8 57
Mandatory food information – Article 9 and 10 58
Ingredients causing allergies or intolerances (Article 9 (1) (c)) 60
Date of minimum durability and use by date (Article 9 (1) (f)) 63
Country of origin and place of provenance (Article 9 (1) (i)) 63
Mandatory nutrition information – Article 9 (1) (l) 65
Additional mandatory particulars – Article 10 and Annex III 67
Presentation of mandatory food information 67
Omission of certain mandatory particulars – Article 16 68
Voluntary food information – Articles 36 and 37 68
The power to impose national measures – Article 39 69
Non-prepacked food – Article 44 70
Practical Application 71
Conclusion 73

Chapter Six	Nutrition and Health Claims	75
	Introduction	75
	Retained EU law and 'EU Exit' Regulations	75
	Authorisations in GB since 1 January 2021	76
	Regulation 1924/2006 – general provisions	78
	Principles for all claims – Article 3	79
	Nutrient profiles – Article 4	80
	General conditions of use	81
	Nutrition claims – specific requirements	82
	Health claims	82
	Restrictions on the use of certain heath claims – Article 12	85
	Types of health claims	85
	Conclusion	86
Chapter Seven	Traceability, Withdrawal and Recalls	89
	Introduction	89
	The retained EU legislation	89
	Types of food incidents	90
	Legal obligations	91
	Practical application – a typical food incident	96
	Incident management teams and plans	101
	Conclusion	102
Chapter Eight	Official Controls and Enforcement	103
	Introduction	103
	Official Controls – Regulation 2017/625	104
	Principles of enforcement	106
	Authorised officers	108
	Powers of authorised officers	109
	Enforcement notices	111
	Responding to enforcement notices	113
	Appealing the notice	113
	Powers of the Magistrates' Court/First-tier Tribunal	114
	Costs	115
	Further appeals	116
	Conclusion	116

Chapter Nine	**Criminal Prosecutions**	117
	Introduction	117
	Food law offences	118
	Commencing a criminal prosecution	119
	Time limits	120
	The investigation and the interview under caution	121
	Challenges to the prosecution case – due diligence	122
	Conclusion	124
Chapter Ten	**Sentencing**	127
	Introduction	127
	The Guideline – general issues	127
	Sentencing of organisations	129
	Sentencing of Individuals	137
	Some points applicable to the sentencing of organisations and individuals	141
	Conclusion	144
Chapter Eleven	**Conclusions and the Future for Food Law in the UK**	147

CHAPTER ONE

FOOD LAW IN THE UK

Introduction

This chapter will briefly explain some of the issues arising from the UK ceasing to be a member of the European Union.

Until 11pm (UK time) on 31 December 2020, the United Kingdom of Great Britain and Northern Ireland was a member of the European Union. This is referred to as IP completion day.

It is not necessary, and would take too much time, to discuss the reasons why the UK decided to leave the EU, but there have been a number of political, social and economic consequences arising from that decision.

This chapter will also briefly review one of the fundamentals of EU law, the free movement of goods.

It will then move to consider how food law is now regulated in the United Kingdom, while recalling that the position in Great Britain (England, Wales and Scotland) is different from the position in Northern Ireland.

The four nations of the United Kingdom

Consumers in each of the four nations of the UK are entitled to the same level of protection from unsafe food and illegal practices as they were when they were EU citizens.

Now that the UK is no longer subject to the EU regulatory regime, the UK authorities have a greater role to play, particularly with regard to developing its own laws and policies and determining applications for approvals and authorisations.

The Food Standards Agency's (FSA) remit covers England, Wales and Northern Ireland and Food Standards Scotland (FSS) has its own separate food law responsibilities and obligations. The FSA and FSS have signed a Memorandum of Understanding (MoU) that sets out the principles for their working relationship.

In its Summary, the MoU states:

"Both the FSA and FSS recognise that each has a contribution to make to an effective food and feed safety regime in the United Kingdom (UK), whilst recognising that their policy, priorities and objectives may not always be identical."

As food is a devolved power, the responsibility for policy and delivery of food controls rests with the authorities in England, Wales, Scotland and Northern Ireland. It is important to have regard to this when considering the rules in each nation.

The UK outside the EU

Since IP completion day, the UK has, from an EU perspective, been classed as a third country without full access to the EU Single Market and the Customs Union.

This has had, and continues to have, significant implications for food businesses and consumers in the UK, and indeed in the EU.

It is now possible for GB (and the UK as a whole subject to the current situation in NI) and the EU to develop their own food laws and policies which may not always be aligned. This is known as regulatory divergence. However, even though that possibility exists, consumer protection must remain the primary focus.

England, Wales and Scotland may also develop their own laws and policies.

One of the comments that made headlines in 2021 was the suggestion that the UK might revert to using imperial, rather than metric units of measurement (for the younger readers, imperial measurements include miles, feet and inches).

Although this may not have meant to signal a definite intention to change the law, it does highlight that GB now has the ability to change laws that it was bound to follow while a Member State of the EU. If you are of more mature years, like myself, you will be reminded of the level of feeling generated by the issue of imperial versus metric units of measurement in the case of *Thoburn v Sunderland City Council and related appeals* [2002] EWHC 195 (Admin).

Irrespective of the legal and political issues, the UK and the EU will remain important trading partners, even if the relationship is currently somewhat strained. However, if the trading rules become more complex or the regulatory landscape becomes too challenging, there will be a temptation, or even a need, to seek new markets. This is already happening with the negotiation and signing of new trade deals.

Applying a holistic approach, regard must be had to the potential adverse impacts on other matters such as food safety, animal welfare and the carbon footprint of this new trade.

Closer to home, the change has also created a line (perhaps a better word than 'border') between GB and NI and some foods must to undergo inspection and checks. This has created political tensions and the UK threatening to "trigger" Article 16 of the Ireland/Northern Ireland Protocol which could effectively suspend the operation of the Protocol.

Article 16, is headed 'Safeguards':

> "1. If the application of this Protocol leads to serious economic, societal or environmental difficulties that are liable to persist, or to diversion of trade, the Union or the United Kingdom may unilaterally take appropriate safeguard measures. Such safeguard measures shall be restricted with regard to their scope and duration to what is strictly necessary in order to remedy the situation. Priority shall be given to such measures as will least disturb the functioning of this Protocol."

It is also worth remembering that the UK's departure from the EU has had a positive impact for some food business, whereas for some it has not made any significant difference.

The free movement of food within the EU

As many GB food businesses use the EU as a route to market, it is worth briefly reviewing what this means.

Food is an international commodity and as such the food businesses and their advisers need access to competent local market advice. While the law in the EU-27 may be the same or similar, it is important to ascertain what the trading conditions are like "on the ground" and how the laws are regulated and enforced by the competent authorities.

In an EU context, the principle of mutual recognition provides that a product lawfully produced or marketed in one EU country may be sold in other Member States without being subject to financial or other barriers. Reference may be made to Regulation 2019/515on the mutual recognition of goods lawfully marketed in another Member State.

This principle arises from the creation of the internal market and the general prohibition on imposing restrictions on imports and exports within the European Union (see for example, Articles 26, 28 and 30 of the Treaty on the Functioning of the European Union (TFEU)).

Member States may not create rules which amount to "quantitative restrictions" on the movement of products (Articles 34 and 35 of the TFEU).

However, prohibitions may be imposed on specified grounds including "the protection of health and life of humans, animals or plants", but this must not amount to a "means of arbitrary discrimination or a disguised restriction on trade between Member States" (Article 36 of the TFEU).

Any attempt to go behind the free movement of goods must be justified, proportionate and for the benefit of consumers.

When assessing the impact of a particular restriction, regard must be had to the product itself and whether or not there are any EU-wide harmonised rules regarding the composition or labelling of the product which apply in the Member States.

For further reading about the principles of mutual recognition, see *Procureur du Roi v Dassonville v S. A. ETS Fourcroy and S. A. Breuval et Cie, Civil Parties (Case 8/74) [1974] 2 C.M.L.R. 436* (Scotch Whisky); *and Rewe-Zentral AG v Bundesmonopolverwaltung für Branntwein (Case 120/78) [1979] 3 C.M.L.R. 494* (French liqueur, 'Cassis de Dijon') and *EC Commission v Spain (Case C-12/00), EC Commission v Italy (Case C-14/00)* (chocolate) and *BS and CA v Ministère public et Conseil nationale de l'ordre des pharmaciens (Case C-633/18* (cannabidiol – CBD).

The free movement of food within the UK

Since IP completion day the rules relating to the movement of goods, including food, between the UK nations have been the responsibility of the UK Government and the devolved nations of England, Wales, Scotland and Northern Ireland.

The rules are contained in the United Kingdom Internal Market Act 2020 which came into force on IP completion day. Goods may be traded freely, with some exceptions, across the UK's internal borders.

This is achieved by two market access principles:

1. The principle of mutual recognition namely goods that may be lawfully sold in the part of the UK in which they were produced or imported into may be sold in the other parts of the UK; and

2. The principle of non-discrimination which prevents the imposition of discriminatory rules in respect of goods with a relevant connection to another part of the UK.

Those market access principles do not apply to:

- Requirements that were in force in a part of the UK before 31 December 2020 and remain unchanged; and to

- Goods sold within Great Britain (England, Scotland and Wales) where requirements are the same across Great Britain

The principles apply with modifications to trade between Great Britain and Northern Ireland, although the provisions of the Northern Ireland Protocol take precedence for as long as the Protocol is in force. This means that any differing requirements on goods sold in Northern Ireland which apply as a result of the Protocol will have to be complied with (i.e. requirements imposed pursuant to EU food law).

The market access principles do not apply in the circumstances set out in schedule 1 to the 2020 Act which includes regulations relating to controlling pests and disease, and unsafe food.

The Internal Markets Act 2020 has a number of twists and turns and should be reviewed in detail.

Northern Ireland

Before looking at the substantive changes required for GB law, it is worth just noting how EU food law continues to apply in NI (the "why" it applies is a different issue). Although EU food law applies in NI, it is not an EU Member State.

One consequence of situation in NI is that there is an open border between Northern Ireland and Ireland. Another consequence is that there are particular issues and restrictions relating to the trade in goods between Northern Ireland and Great Britain.

EU food law applies in Northern Ireland as a result of the Withdrawal Agreement and the Protocol on Ireland/Northern Ireland.

Article 5 (4) of the Protocol states that those EU laws set out in Annex 2 apply to Northern Ireland.

The Annex contains more than 40 different sections covering a wide-range of goods, each one setting out the particular EU legal provisions.

Some of the food law provisions listed in Annex 2 that apply in Northern Ireland are:

- Food – general (includes Regulation 178/2002 (and confirming that the term Member State in Article 29 does not include NI), Regulation 1169/2011 and Regulation 1924/2006)

- Food – hygiene (includes Regulation 852/2004 and Regulation 853/2004)

- Food – ingredients, traces, residues, marketing standards (includes the regulations on food additives, Directive 2002/46 and Regulation 609/2013)

- Food contact material (includes Regulation 1935/2004)

- Feed – products and hygiene (includes Regulation 767/2009, Regulation 1831/2003 and Regulation 183/2005)

- GMOs (includes Regulation 1829/2003)

- Animal welfare (includes Regulation 1/2005 and Regulation 1099/2009)

- Official controls (includes Regulation 2017/625)

The continued impact of EU food law in Great Britain

When it was a member of the EU, the UK was bound by all aspects of EU food law. EU food regulations had direct effect and EU food directives had to be transposed by the Member State in a way that gave effect to their meaning and purpose.

As the majority of EU food legislation are regulations, when it was a Member State the UK had little to do other than enacting legislation dealing with matters such as identifying the competent authority, deciding how the law would be regulated and enforced, and deciding what sanctions should be available for non-compliance.

Upon leaving the EU, it would have been impossible for the UK authorities to create a whole new 'statute book' of food law for GB.

In general terms, the solution was:

a) To keep the version of EU food law (which was primarily in the form of regulations) that was in force in the UK at IP completion day (31 December 2020); and

b) To amend that EU food law and existing GB food laws that gave effect to those and other EU laws such as directives

This created a new category of domestic law known as 'retained EU law' which includes:

1. Direct EU legislation

This includes EU law that was directly applicable in the UK such as regulations and decisions.

For example, Regulation 178/2002, the general food law regulation and Regulation 852/2004 on the hygiene of foodstuffs.

The English language version of the EU law is authoritative.

2. EU-derived domestic legislation

Domestic legislation made under section 2 (2) of the European Communities Act 1972 and other domestic legislation giving effect to EU obligations.

For example, the Food Supplements (England) Regulations 2003 which transposed Directive 2002/46 but which have themselves been amended for example by EU Exit Regulations (see below).

3. Retained case law and retained general principles of EU law

This includes principles set out by, and decisions of, the Court of Justice of the European Union that had effect on IP completion day in relation to the above categories.

It also retains general EU principles such as proportionality and decisions of domestic courts and tribunals relating to the above categories.

In addition, the following should be noted:

1. The European Communities Act 1972, under which EU law was 'supreme' in the UK has been repealed.

2. Although UK courts can no longer seek a ruling from the Court of Justice of the European Union (Article 267 of the TFEU), that court retains jurisdiction to hear and determine any questions that had been referred to it prior to 31 December 2020 – Article 86 (2) of the Withdrawal Agreement and see the case of The Queen on the application of the *Association of Independent Meat Suppliers and another v Food Standards Agency* (Case C-579/19 a Judgment of the CJEU dated 2 September 2021)

Although, revisions to EU food law post 31 December 2020 do not apply in the UK, that does not mean that domestic law and policy has not moved forward. The final chapter reviews some domestic laws that have been, or are due to be, enacted.

Making food law relevant to and applicable in GB – EU Exit Regulations

The main way in which food law was revised to take account of the UK's departure from the EU was to enact a series of statutory instruments to amend the retained EU food law regulations themselves and the GB legislation that gave effect to EU food laws (e.g. regulations and directives).

The many thousands of statutory instruments that enacted these changes generally contain the words "EU Exit" in their titles.

However, although this was a basically sound approach to resolving the difficulties arising from the UK's departure from the EU, searching for and successfully finding the applicable "EU Exit" Regulations is not always straightforward.

Further, some EU Exit Regulations were passed in 2019 and they refer to the UK. Once, an agreement between the UK and EU had been reached regarding their future relationship, those 2019 Regulations had to be amended to reflect the different positions of GB and NI and to provide for the identification of the GB competent authorities.

In addition, it is not always as straightforward as taking a word or phrase from the EU or existing UK law (such as food supplements) and using that as a search term to obtain the applicable EU Exit regulation.

Websites such as www.legislation.gov.uk provide resources for finding EU Exit regulations as well as EU and domestic legislation as retained EU law. There are some web resources and paid subscription services which provide amended and consolidated versions of EU retained law and are very helpful.

For the power to make regulations giving effect to the UK (GB)'s departure reference may be made to the European Union (Withdrawal) Act 2018 and European Union (Withdrawal Agreement) Act 2020. The need for revised legislation was to deal with "deficiencies arising from withdrawal" (see section 8 of the 2018 Act).

The new legislation is complex and finding the particular provision that amends pre-IP completion day law can be quite laborious.

EU Exit Regulations – an example

It may assist to provide a brief example of how GB food law looks since IP completion day. The Nutrition (Amendment etc.) (EU Exit) Regulations 2019 (2019 No. 651) and the Nutrition (Amendment etc.) (EU Exit) Regulations 2020 (2020 No. 1476) may be used for this purpose.

Jurisdictional application

1) The 2019 Regulations were enacted along with equivalent regulations for Wales, Scotland and Northern Ireland;

2) The original version of the 2019 Regulations applied to the United Kingdom but as a consequence of NI remaining part of the EU, the 2020 Regulations made an amendment so the 2019 Regulations now apply to England, Wales and Scotland (regulation 1);

Subject-matter amendment – food supplements

3) The 2019 Regulations, as amended, make particular provisions about food supplements. This means that searching for "food supplements" and "EU Exit Regulations" will not necessarily be sufficient find the Regulations that give effect to the changes;

4) The general effect of the Regulations is to transfer the regulation of food supplements from the EU institutions, initially to the authorities in the UK and then to those in GB;

5) Under the original 2019 Regulations (regulation 5), the power to make regulations in respect of food supplements is exercisable by the "appropriate authority" which is defined as;

   (a) for regulations applying in relation to England, the Secretary of State;

   (b) for regulations applying in relation to Scotland, the Scottish Ministers;

   (c) for regulations applying in relation to Wales, the Welsh Ministers;

   (d) for regulations applying in relation to Northern Ireland, the Department of Health

   The reference to Northern Ireland was omitted from IP completion day.

6) Schedules 1 and 2 to the 2019 Regulations provide the list of vitamins and minerals that may be used in the manufacture of food supplements and allows for the amendment of those schedules and relating to food supplements placed on the market in GB;

   It can be seen that these provisions replicate, certainly at present, the provisions of EU directive 2002/46 on food supplements that continues to applies in EU 27 and NI.

7) Regulations 3 and 4 of the 2019 Regulations provide for regulations to be made in GB in relation to purity criteria and for setting maximum amounts of vitamins and minerals that may be present in food supplements;

8) Regulation 12 of the 2019 Regulations also make substantive amendments to the Food Supplements (England) Regulations 2003;

   a) The definitions in Directive 2001/83 (medicinal products) and Directive 2002/46 (food supplements) are omitted,

   b) The definition of medicinal product is now as set out in the Human Medicines Regulations 2012 rather than the definition in Directive 2001/83 (medicinal products),

   c) References to the list of vitamins and minerals permitted for use in food supplements in Annex I and Annex II of Directive 2002/46 are now to be found in schedule 1 and schedule 2 of the 2019 Regulations (see above)

<u>Subject-matter amendment – other</u>

9) The Regulations also make provision for the amendment of;

   a) Several pieces of domestic legislation including; medical foods, Kava-kava in food, the addition of vitamins, minerals and other substances in food, infant formula and food for specific groups;

   b) EU Regulations in force in GB as retained EU law including; Regulation 1924/2006 on nutrition and health claims, Regulation 1925/2006 on the addition of vitamins and minerals and other substances to food and Regulation 609/2013 on food for specific groups; and

   c) Various Commission Regulations in force in GB as retained EU law, for example by omitting references to "Community" or "Union" as appropriate and inserting references to Great Britain.

Interpreting food law

EU food law is enacted following a process that involves the Parliament (the peoples' representatives), the Commission (the EU "civil service"), the Council (ministers from the Member States), the Court of Justice of the European Union (interpreting EU law) and the European Food Safety Authority (providing advice on scientific issues).

EU law has to be relevant to and have regard to the now 447+ million EU citizens with their differing needs, requirements, language, culture and history. This can result in a law based on compromise which the national institutions must then interpret, apply and enforce.

Interpreting EU law requires a careful assessment of the wording of the legal provision but also, and of particular relevance for food law, by having regard to the context in which the law occurs and the objectives pursued by the rules of which it is part (see for example *Merck* Case 292/82, and *Verband Sozialer Wettwerb eV v Innova GmbH* Case C-19/15). This often means going beyond the mere "letter of the law".

For further reading in relation to interpretation of hygiene laws in an EU context see the decisions of the Court of Justice of the European Union in *Albrecht and others Case C-382/10, 6 October 2011* (containers for self-service retail of bread and bakery products) and *Astrid Preissl Case C-381/10 (*the installation of a washbasin in food premises). They are discussed further in chapter 4 on food hygiene.

In a domestic context, the High Court has confirmed the above position concerning interpreting EU law; "when interpreting these [food hygiene] Regulations, it is necessary to have regard to the purpose for which they were created, namely, to protect consumers with regard to food hygiene." (*Kothari, Naik and Raw Lasan Ltd v London Borough of Harrow [2009] EWHC 1354 (Admin)*)

As the primary focus of food law in GB continues to be the safety of food and the protection of consumers, there is no reason to believe that this general approach to statutory interpretation will change in the short term.

However, the interpretation of law in a post-EU environment is not always straightforward and further guidance can be found in domestic case law such as *Lipton v BA City Flyer Limited [2021] EWCA Civ 254.*

Conclusion

The UK's decision to leave the EU has undoubtedly created challenges for the food industry and for consumers.

At present, November 2021, it is very hard to assess the real impact of that decision due to the ongoing impact of Covid-19.

The problems in the food supply chain that have been experienced during the past year might be due to the pandemic, or to the UK leaving the EU or to both. Until the issues relating to Covid-19 are resolved, the true level of change resulting from the UK being outside the EU may not be known.

Of course, the issues directly linked to the UK's departure from the EU might well have been resolved, or almost resolved, by the time the pandemic has ended (although as at November 2021 there is little sign of and end to the pandemic).

CHAPTER TWO

THE REGULATION OF FOOD BUSINESSES AND FOODSTUFFS

Introduction

Food business establishments must either be registered or approved depending on the type of foods they handle.

Certain foods must be authorised before they may be placed on the market. In other cases, some aspect of the food or its presentation requires particular control, such as health claims.

As we have seen, the UK legal and regulatory regime for foods differs between Great Britain and Northern Ireland. Nevertheless, an individual food may still need to be regulated in some way.

This chapter reviews the rules relating to registration and approval, which have not changed significantly since the UK left the EU, and the rules relating to the authorisation of foods and the regulation of food related matters.

Registration and approval of food businesses

In general terms, a food business will either register with the competent authority (e.g. a restaurant registers with the local authority in whose area the business operates) or it requires approval from the competent authority (e.g. a slaughterhouse requiring approval from the Food Standards Agency).

Registration is done by completing a food business registration form. This tells the competent authority, the local council for example, that the business is operating in its area and provides information about the activities taking place (what type of food is being sold, is it mainly prepacked and/or is on-site production taking place). The FBO must submit the registration form prior to commencing business but does not have to wait for permission before it can start trading. The business must thereafter notify the authority if there is "any significant change in activities" or if the establishment closes down (Article 6 of Regulation 852/2004 on the Hygiene of Foodstuffs).

An "establishment" is any unit of a food business (Article 2 of Regulation 852/2004).

The competent authority will add the establishment to its list of food premises to be inspected in accordance with its own policy. The frequency of inspection is related to the level of risk created by the type of activity taking place (a small retailer selling mainly prepackaged food is likely to have fewer hazards and therefore will have a lower risk profile than a retailer operating a scratch bakery or other on-site food production activities).

Registration is generally not required for establishments where food is handled occasionally. The test for registration is referrable to the degree of organisation and continuity of activities. Someone who handles, prepares, stores or serves food occasionally and on a small scale may not be considered as an 'undertaking'.

Even if registration is not required, some of the general provisions of food law will still apply to the food (for example ensuring only safe food is placed on the market).

Further information can be found in paragraph 2.12.6 of the Food Standards Agency's Food Law Practice Guidance (England) (Issued March 2021).

This issue has become more noticeable in connection with charitable organisations providing food for the homeless and others in need. If this is carried out with any degree of regularity and organisation (both of which may well apply), those in charge will be required to register as a food business. This may not have been foreseen when the activity commenced, but there is always a balance between protecting consumers, who in this situation may be particularly vulnerable, and not imposing what might be seen as excessive requirements on people trying to make a difference.

Food businesses that handle products of animal origin must obtain prior approval from the relevant competent authority where this is required by Regulation 853/2004 (e.g. the FSA). This is a formal process in which the FBO, its premises and its activities are inspected and only if everything is in order will approval be given. The FBO cannot begin trading unless and until approval is given and this may be conditional or final.

The 'threat' of the approval being suspended or revoked may be used as an incentive to ensure that the FBO remains compliant with their obligations.

Businesses that only need to register may have very infrequent contact with officials from their competent authority. However, business requiring approval may be supervised by Official Veterinarians (OVs) who are present whenever the activities are taking place (e.g. slaughtering of animals) and the OV may report issues of non-compliance to the business operator, and also to the competent authority, as and when they occur which could be on a daily basis.

EFSA – now GB expert committees and appropriate authorities

The European Food Safety Authority (EFSA) plays a significant role in the provision of scientific opinions on matters relating to food safety and consumer protection.

An example of this is in its scientific assessment of proposed health claims, but this role no longer applies in GB. The Nutrition (Amendment etc.) (EU Exit) Regulations 2019 (2019 No. 651) (see above) make appropriate amendments to Regulation 1924/2006 on nutrition and health claims by substituting:

'Authority' means the European Food Safety Authority established by Regulation (EC) No 178/2002.

with:

'expert committee' means a committee with appropriate expertise in the matter to be considered, approved by an appropriate authority to give advice for the purposes of this Regulation;"

The "appropriate authority" is; in England, the Secretary of State; in Scotland, the Scottish Ministers; in Wales, the Welsh Ministers.

Products requiring authorisation

Many foods require some form of control or authorisation. It is not possible to mention them all here but they include:

- Food flavourings;
- Food additives;
- Food enzymes;
- Genetically modified organisms;
- Novel foods; and
- Feed additives

At EU level, the requirement for authorisation and the criteria necessary to obtain authorisation are set out in the product-specific legislation.

The procedure for obtaining authorisations is too complex to be covered in this book, but it may involve the European Food Safety Authority undertaking a risk assessment and then providing an opinion on the safety of the substance in question.

If all goes well and the food or substance is deemed to be safe, the EU authorisation procedure results in it being placed on a positive list contained in an EU law and it may be used in food, but may be subject to conditions of use.

The EFSA and the EU authorisation approval regime is no longer applicable in Great Britain, although this is still route to obtain a new authorisation for products being placed on the market in Northern Ireland.

As was noted in the Preface, EFSA may be called upon to re-evaluate a food or substance as was the case in May 2021 with Titanium Dioxide (E 171) when it determined that it was no longer safe to be used as a food additive. Legislation was introduced to ban the use of the substance.

Placing a product requiring authorisation on the market in Great Britain

The responsibility for authorising products in Great Britain now falls to the Food Standards Agency (FSA) and Food Standards Scotland (FSS).

The following is a brief guide to the process for products requiring authorisation. Reference should be made to the specific legislation and guidance for particular product types. There is additional guidance for authorisation applications for CBD products.

<u>Application</u>

The initial application form is submitted on line via the FSA's regulated products' webpages.

Once this has been submitted, the applicant receives an application number and a secure link for the uploading of the applicable supporting documents.

<u>Information to be provided</u>

This will depend on the type of product in respect of which authorisation is being sought.

However, the application dossier will generally comprise:

- Administrative information – e.g. the name of the applicant and a contact person
- Technical information – e.g. information about the product or process (including if any information is confidential)

- Scientific information – to enable a thorough risk assessment

The process for a new authorisation

Once the FSA is satisfied that the application contains all the required information, a risk assessment will be undertaken. This will be done by one of the FSA's Joint Expert Groups (Animal Feed and Feed Additives, Additives, Enzymes and other regulated products or Food Contact Materials) and/or one of the Scientific Advisory Committees (e.g. Toxicity, Microbiological Safety, Novel Foods or Animal Feedingstuffs).

In addition to the formal risk assessment, the authorisation process has regard to a number of other factors relevant to the particular product and/or food safety risk including:

- Impact on the environment, animal welfare and food security;

- Likely consumer behaviours in response to risk and emerging trends;

- The economic impact of the risk, the costs and benefit of implementing risk management options and who will bear the cost; and

- Technical considerations such as scientific and technological advances and the ability to enforce and verify controls

Once all the evidence has been obtained, a recommendation is made to ministers who then decide whether to authorise the product for use in Great Britain. If authorisation is granted, the relevant legislation will be updated along with the register of authorised products.

A consultation exercise allowing comments to be made about the application takes place during the authorisation process.

Ongoing applications and existing authorisations

If an authorisation was submitted under the EU regime prior to 31 December 2020, this will need to be submitted to the FSA (the initial on-line application form asks – "Have you previously submitted this application for approval in the European Union?").

The FSA may have regard to any published EFSA opinion and/or the outcome of any risk management discussions that occurred prior to 31 December 2020.

However, as the responsibility for authorisation has now moved away from the EU to the GB authorities, they may decide to undertake their own full risk assessment.

If prior to 31 December 2020 the product had been fully authorised by the European Commission and the applicable legislation was in force, then this authorisation remains valid for GB.

Full details on the authorisation process are available on the Regulated Products section of the FSA website and further guidance can be obtained by contacting regulatedproducts@food.gov.uk

The register of regulated product applications

The register is publicly available and contains information such as the name of the applicant, the product name, the product type and the phase reached in the assessment process.

Product types in the register include novel food, feed additives, food contact material and food additives.

The phases of the assessment process as recorded in the register are:

- Risk assessment – one of the Joint Expert Groups and/or Scientific Advisory Committees decide if the product is safe to be placed on the market in England, Wales and Scotland

- Risk management – consideration of possible risk management options and making a recommendation to ministers

- Authorisation decision pending – the final stage of the assessment process where ministers decide whether to authorised the product for use on Great Britain.

Conclusion

It is no surprise that GB has continued the requirement for authorisation of certain foods. The process is similar to the previous approach and will continue see the risk assessment process placing safety as its primary consideration.

It will take some time to see how the GB process works in practice and whether there are any new issues or approaches that apply to this new procedure.

It will be interesting to see whether the processes in GB and the EU remains broadly comparable or whether one or the other applies different criteria for assessing the same type of product. This could lead to product A or claim B being authorised in GB but not in the EU and vice versa.

Products for the Northern Irish market continue to be considered for authorisation under the EU procedure.

CHAPTER THREE

FOOD SAFETY

Introduction

As expected, food safety remains the priority for GB food competent authorities; as the saying goes, if it is not safe, it is not food.

There are many food related issues for legislators and regulators in the EU, UK (GB) and globally such as sustainability, security, the impact of climate change, reducing the carbon footprint, single use plastics and food waste.

No matter what action is taken to pursue those policies, the one that must not be downgraded is the fundamental objective of ensuring the food we eat is safe.

While the content of the law may have changed, the "day-to-day" activities involved in producing safe food remain the same.

It would be difficult for a food business to seek to explain or justify a food poisoning incident by saying that it was confused about the array of retained EU law and/or the impact of EU Exit regulations.

As a reminder, EU food law regulations that apply in GB as retained EU law are those versions that were in force and applicable in the UK on IP completion day (11 pm 31 December 2020).

Retained EU food law and the 'EU Exit' Regulations

Retained EU law

Regulation 178/2002

Regulation 178/2002 has been amended since IP completion day resulting in consolidated versions dated 27 March 2021 and then 26 May

2021. The revised EU regulation continues to apply in NI, but not in GB.

Domestic law

EU Regulation 178/2002 has effect in England by virtue of the Food Safety and Hygiene (England) Regulations 2013 as amended. There are similar food safety laws applicable in Wales and Scotland.

The 'EU Exit' Regulations

The General Food Law (Amendment etc.) (EU Exit) Regulations 2019 (2019 No. 641)

As amended by the

Food and Feed Hygiene and Safety (Miscellaneous Amendments etc.) (EU Exit) Regulations 2020 (2020 No. 1504)

One example of the amendments required to make Regulation 178/2002 applicable to GB can be seen in Article 11 of that Regulation (Food and feed imported into the Community).

The EU version states:

> "**Food and feed imported into the Community**
>
> Food and feed imported into the Community for placing on the market within the Community shall comply with the relevant requirements of food law or conditions recognised by the Community to be at least equivalent thereto or, where a specific agreement exists between the Community and the exporting country, with requirements contained therein."

This has been amended to read:

> "**Food and feed imported into Great Britain**
>
> Food and feed imported into Great Britain for placing on the market within Great Britain must comply with the relevant

requirements of food law or conditions recognised by Great Britain to be at least equivalent thereto or, where a specific agreement exists between the United Kingdom and an exporting country, with requirements contained therein."

It should also be noted that other significant parts of Regulation 178/2002 have been revised by the EU Exit Regulations:

- Chapter 3 dealing with EFSA has been repealed;

- Chapter 4 dealing with the Rapid Alert System, Crisis Management and Emergencies has been repealed, except for Article 53 which has been amended to apply to emergency measures where food or feed originating in the United Kingdom, or imported into Great Britain from outside the United Kingdom "is likely to constitute a serious risk to human health, animal health or the environment".

  In such a case the appropriate authority may take appropriate action such as suspending the placing on the market of the food or suspending the import of the food. The appropriate authority is defined in the amended Article 2 of 178/2002 as; England, the Secretary of State; Wales, the Welsh Ministers; and Scotland, the Scottish Ministers.

The UK no longer has full access to RASFF (the Rapid Alert System for Food and Feed) but continues to receive specific alerts affecting the UK. This does not mean that it has no way of playing its part when food incidents occur as the UK has access to INFOSAN (International Food Safety Authority Network).

The principles of food safety

<u>The retained Regulation 178/2002 – some basic concepts</u>

The following contains definitions which still apply in GB but with necessary amendments (some of which, but not all, I have indicated by crossing through words that have been deleted).

Care should be taken to cross reference aspects of the domestic and EU law with the corresponding parts of the EU Exit Regulations to see whether an amendment has been made and if so, what the effect of the change.

Scope (Article 1) and general application (Article 4)

The twin principles of the Regulation are; "a high level of protection of human health and consumers' interests in relation to food", and "ensuring the effective functioning of the ~~internal~~ market".

The word "internal" before market appears in the EU version but not in the retained version applicable in GB.

The regulation applies generally to all stages of production, processing and distribution of food, and also of feed produced for, or fed to, food-producing animals.

Food (Article 2)

The definition of food (also described as "foodstuff") is:

> *"any substance or product, whether processed, partially processed or unprocessed, intended to be, or reasonably expected to be ingested by humans".*

This includes; drink, chewing gum and any substance incorporated into the food during its manufacture, preparation or treatment, but excludes; feed, live animals (unless prepared for placing on the market for human consumption), plants prior to harvesting, medicinal products, cosmetics, tobacco, narcotic or psychotropic substances, and residues and contaminants.

Objectives (Article 5 and Article 8)

The main objectives of food law include; a high level of protection of human life and health and the protection of consumers' interests, including fair practices in food trade. Food law should allow consumers to make informed choices in relation to the foods they consume.

Food business operator (Article 3 and Article 17)

The food business operator (FBO) is "the natural or legal persons responsible for ensuring that the requirements of food law are met within the business under their control".

Establishing the identity of the correct FBO is a matter of law and fact. Questions of control and/or the extent of control over particular aspects of the food business may be important as they point towards different FBOs.

The FBO may be a company and/or an individual, and as was said at paragraph 21 of the judgment in *The Queen on the Application of Rasool v Tower Bridge Magistrates' Court [2013] EWHC 4736 (Admin)* "it is clearly right that it is possible in law for there to be more than one FBO".

Food law (Article 3)

This means the laws, regulations and administrative provisions governing food in general, and food safety in particular, ~~whether at Community or national level;~~ it covers any stage of production, processing and distribution of food, and also of feed produced for, or fed to, food-producing animals. (words crossed out are deleted in the retained EU law)

Placing on the market (Article 3)

This is much wider than sale or supply and is defined as;

> *"the holding of food or feed for the purpose of sale, including offering for sale or any other form of transfer, whether free of charge or not, and the sale, distribution, and other forms of transfer themselves".*

The phrase can be seen in the prohibition in Article 14; "food shall not be placed on the market if it is unsafe".

Food business (Article 3)

Any undertaking, whether for profit or not and whether public or private, carrying out any of the activities related to any stage of production, processing and distribution of food. The concept of "undertakings" in food law is based on an assessment of the degree and level of organisation of the activities (see the discussion about this issue in chapter 2).

Stages of production, processing and distribution (Article 3)

The definitions of food law and food business refer to obligations at any stages of production, processing and distribution. This means;

> *"any stage, including import, from and including the primary production of a food, up to and including its storage, transport, sale or supply to the final consumer and, where relevant, the importation, production, manufacture, storage, transport, distribution, sale and supply of feed".*

Hazard and risk (Articles 3 and 6)

In order to effectively protect consumers, food law is based on risk analysis. Enforcement should be guided by the same principle.

A hazard is "a biological, chemical or physical agent in or condition of food or feed with the potential to cause an adverse health effect".

Risk is "a function of the probability of an adverse health effect and the severity of that risk, *consequential to* a hazard" (my emphasis).

There must therefore be a hazard before there can be a risk and if there is no hazard, there is no risk. This point might be relevant when deciding how, or if, to challenge any enforcement action which may be based on the assessment of an individual officer (see chapter 8).

Food safety (Article 14)

Article 14 (1) is quite clear; "food shall not be placed on the market if it is unsafe".

<u>Unsafe food (Article 14 (2))</u>

Food is deemed to be unsafe if it is considered to be injurious to health and/or unfit for human consumption.

Determining unsafe food (Article 14 (3))

In determining whether any food is unsafe, regard shall be had:

(a) to the normal conditions of use of the food by the consumer and at each stage of production, processing and distribution, and

(b) to the information provided to the consumer, including information on the label, or other information generally available to the consumer concerning the avoidance of specific adverse health effects from a particular food or category of foods.

A couple of points may usefully be made here.

Raw meat is, usually, unsafe to eat. The 'normal conditions of use' have regard to the need to cook meat properly in order to remove the hazard. Removing the hazard removes the risk.

Article 14 (3) (b) might apply to a food containing an ingredient causing an allergy or intolerance.

Injurious to health (Article 14 (4))

In determining whether any food is injurious to health, regard shall be had:

(a) not only to the probable immediate and/or short-term and/or long-term effects of that food on the health of a person consuming it, but also on subsequent generations;

(b) to the probable cumulative toxic effects;

(c) to the particular health sensitivities of a specific category of consumers where the food is intended for that category of consumers.

Article 14 (4) (c) might apply to a food that is marketed as being suitable for coeliacs but which contains gluten.

Unfit for human consumption (Article 14 (5))

In determining whether food is unfit for human consumption, regard shall be had to whether the food is unacceptable for human consumption according to its intended use, for reasons of contamination, whether by extraneous matter or otherwise, or through putrefaction, deterioration or decay.

Unfitness might equate to food being "unacceptable" which might occur due to extensive mould or to unexpected organoleptic properties such as strong taints, odours or tastes, or food containing hair, a plaster or a fingernail.

Depending on the type and/or quantity of the extraneous matter, the same food might be both injurious to health and unfit for human consumption.

Food in a batch (Article 14 (6))

Where any food which is unsafe is part of a batch, lot or consignment of food, it is presumed that all the food in that batch, lot or consignment is also unsafe, unless following a detailed assessment there is no evidence that the rest of the batch, lot or consignment is unsafe.

Where the competent authority has shown, after proper sampling and analysis, that some of the food is unsafe, it can then rely on the presumption that all the food is unsafe. Unless the FBO samples and analyses other products from the batch and shows they are not unsafe, the whole consignment is likely to be detained and destroyed.

The FBO must consider their options carefully and their response will depend on all the circumstances. If the problem has been traced to an unsafe ingredient that the FBO knows has been used in all the food in the consignment, there may be little point in obtaining costly analysis in order to try and displace the presumption. As consumer safety is paramount, the FBO often faces an uphill struggle to persuade the competent authority, or a court, that the presumption should not apply.

The financial value of the consignment, the shelf-life of the product, the cost and resources required to test product and the need to fulfil a particular order may be relevant to how the FBO responds to the consignment being detained because some food within the consignment has been shown to be unsafe.

Food in compliance with specific provisions (Articles 14 (7) and (8))

Food that complies with specific legislation in force in the relevant constituent territory of Great Britain governing food safety shall be deemed to be safe insofar as the aspects covered by the specific provisions are concerned.

It should be noted that Article 14 (8) allows competent authorities to take action to impose restrictions on a food being placed on the market or to require its withdrawal from the market where there are reasons to suspect that, despite being in conformity with the applicable provisions, the food is unsafe.

Any decisions or actions would focus on the need to protect consumer health and would only be taken following a detailed risk assessment.

Practical application – a case of food poisoning

Consuming unsafe food may lead to serious illness and, in the worst-case scenario, death (most notably in the case of a severe allergic reaction).

Investigations involving the placing on the market of alleged unsafe food may engage the services of the Public Analyst, the Government Chemist or other appropriately accredited laboratories or suitably qualified experts. Samples taken from food, humans, premises and animals might need to be analysed and the results explained.

In every case where legal proceedings are taken or contemplated, all parties should have regard to the rules around sampling and all appropriate evidential rules, particularly in relation to the gathering, recording, handling and transferring of samples and other evidence.

Although it may appear "obvious" that a foodstuff was unsafe, had been "clearly supplied" by the business under investigation and the food "must have" caused an illness, the party asserting this must be able to prove this to the appropriate evidential standard. The other party should check and test the evidence presented by the other side (i.e. the competent authority or an individual consumer).

The consequences for consumers eating unsafe food may depend on a variety of factors including their age and general health, the source and cause of the illness and the amount of the harmful pathogen that has been consumed.

Investigating, prosecuting and defending food poisoning cases in the criminal and civil courts is not always straightforward. In every case a thorough and detailed enquiry must be made by all parties. Evidence to prove or disprove liability is required and sometimes it is necessary to look beyond what might, at first glance, appear to be the obvious, or only, cause of the problem. Nothing should be presumed or taken for granted.

The following issues may be relevant issues to be investigated and proved.

- The source

  The contamination may be due to salmonella, Escherichia coli (E. coli) or norovirus.

- The cause

  Food can become contaminated at any stage of production, processing or cooking. For example, it could become be contaminated due to incorrect cooking, handling, storing or reheating. Food consumed past its "use-by date" could be the culprit. The food could have become contaminated from within the food premises but any contamination could have occurred after it had been purchased by the consumer (for example by being stored incorrectly).

- Symptoms

  Symptoms may be minor (some pain and sickness resolving within a day or two, with or without medical consultation/intervention), moderate (where the symptoms are worse or more extensive and lasts for days requiring medical intervention), severe (leading to more extensive medical intervention, such as hospital admission) or fatal (where death is caused by or contributed to by having consumed the unsafe food).

- Notification to the food business operator

  The FBO might become aware of the problem in many ways; direct contact from consumers and/or the competent authority which may provide specific information about the problem (e.g. when the alleged food poisoning occurred, the possible 'suspect' foods, who was affected etc.) and this may assist the FBO to investigate the situation. Alternatively, initial knowledge may come indirectly via social media which can make the situation more difficult to manage.

  The FBO will immediately carry out their own investigation and take such steps as are necessary to protect consumers (e.g. by destroying affected product or quarantining all the 'suspect' foods pending further investigation).

  The FBO may need to undertake urgent works such as a deep clean of the premises and equipment, reviewing its food safety management system, revising it where necessary and retraining staff.

- The investigation by the competent authorities

  Investigating a food poisoning outbreak may involve multi-disciplinary meetings at which all the relevant agencies (e.g. food competent authorities, public health organisations, health protection teams and medical practitioners) will identify and monitor the scale and extent of the problem. Even before a meeting has taken place, this may involve communicating with consumers, other competent authorities, FBOs and health professionals. In a widespread serious case where speed of notification of the risk to consumers is important, this may require communication via television, print media, the internet and social media.

The investigation may involve taking samples from:

- People who have been ill (e.g. stool samples);
- From the suspect food (if it is available or from food from a similar batch, if possible);
- From the food premises (e.g. from equipment used to prepare the food or work surfaces); and
- Possibly from animals (e.g. if it is suspected that the initial source of the contamination occurred at a farm or market).

The complainants will be asked to complete a food history questionnaire which records information about the food they had consumed over a period of time prior to the onset of illness.

The aim of the investigation is to try and identify a particular food or foods and/or location common to all, or to a significant number of, the complainants.

The FBO(s) under suspicion will be spoken to by the officials from the competent authority as part of the evidence gathering process and the FBO will wish to cooperate with the investigation. However, it is important that the FBO seeks legal advice early in the investigation and obtains guidance about how they should interact with the relevant authorities, particularly if the FBO, or members of staff, are being questioned or if they are requested to attend an interview under caution during which the competent authority will seek to obtain evidence for use in court proceedings.

- Legal action

The competent authority may take action to immediately close the premises which are suspected to be implicated in the food poisoning, or example by means of Hygiene Emergency Prohibition Notice and/or to detain foods.

After a full review of the evidence, the authority may decide to bring criminal proceedings and/or the injured parties may bring civil actions seeking damages for personal injury. Both of these may be very costly for the FBO in terms of financial outlay (not all of which may be covered by insurance), resources and staff time and in damaging from a public relations perspective.

- <u>Some other points to note</u>

  Legal proceedings must be based on the sufficiency of admissible evidence (e.g. from complainants, environmental health officers, health professionals, scientists and other experts) to prove the case to the appropriate legal standard of proof ("beyond reasonable doubt" in a criminal prosecution and "on the balance of probabilities" in civil proceedings).

  During the official investigation, the officers should keep all their work under review to ensure that they are obtaining all the relevant evidence and doing so in the correct way. This might include taking samples, continuity of obtaining, storing, handing and transmitting evidence, correct use of the caution when questioning FBOs and others, using competent, appropriate and accredited laboratories and obtaining evidence from everyone who is involved in the case.

  If this is not done at the appropriate time during the investigative process it may not be possible to 'fill any evidential gaps' later on. If there are gaps then they will be identified and exploited by the opposing party and their advisers.

Conclusion

Food safety is very often linked to poor hygiene practices (see the next chapter). Consumers can be kept safe by providing information about ingredients, correct procedures for cooking and storing food and by providing accurate use-by dates.

In summary, when advising on food safety issues, including food poisoning cases, it is important to recall the basic definitions of food law, where is the hazard, does this create a risk to health and if so, how?

Never take anything for granted, challenge the evidence (within reason and only when appropriate to do so) and always bear in mind that the cause of any illness may not be due to any fault on the part of the FBO or the evidence may not be sufficient to prove fault.

CHAPTER FOUR

FOOD HYGIENE

Introduction

Poor food hygiene practices may be linked to the provision of unsafe food. On the other side of the coin, good food hygiene practices, complemented by a positive food safety culture can avoid, or at least significantly reduce, the risks of supplying unsafe food and other non-compliances that can be detrimental to a food business.

In addition to the laws covered in this chapter, Regulation (EC) No 2073/2005 on microbiological criteria for foods is relevant as a means of checking the suitability and acceptability of foods and processes. It lays down food safety criteria for relevant foodborne bacteria, their toxins and metabolites, such as *Salmonella*, *Listeria monocytogenes*, *Enterobacter sakazakii*, *staphylococcal enterotoxins* and *histamine* in specific foods. It also lays down certain process hygiene criteria to indicate the correct functioning of the production process.

Arguably the most common interaction between food law and criminal law involves prosecutions for breaches of food hygiene regulations (which may include prosecutions for placing unsafe food on the market).

Food hygiene cases are likely to receive media attention particularly where the food business is well-known or where there is some "interesting" element to the case such as evidence of the presence of rodents in the food premises or, as happened in 2021, illegally cutting meat at a car wash.

In addition to prosecutions, breaches of food hygiene laws often feature highly in relation to the grounds for taking enforcement action such as issuing as Hygiene Emergency Prohibition Notices.

Retained EU food law and the 'EU Exit' Regulations

General hygiene requirements

Retained EU law

Regulation 852/2004

Domestic law

The Food Safety and Hygiene (England) Regulations 2013 and similar laws in Wales and Scotland

EU Exit Regulations

General Food Law (Amendment etc.) (EU Exit) Regulations 2019 (2019 No. 641)

General Food Hygiene (Amendment) (EU Exit) Regulations 2019 (2019 No. 642)

As amended by the

Food and Feed Hygiene and Safety (Miscellaneous Amendments etc.) (EU Exit) Regulations 2020 (2020 No. 1504)

Specific hygiene rules for food of animal origin

Retained EU law

Regulation 853/2004

Domestic law

The Official Feed and Food Controls (England) Regulations 2009 and similar regulations in Wales and Scotland.

EU Exit Regulations

The Specific Food Hygiene (Amendment etc.) (EU Exit) Regulations 2019

The Food and Feed Hygiene and Safety (Miscellaneous Amendments etc.) (EU Exit) Regulations 2020

A particular change to Regulation 852/2004 in the EU

Before considering some of the hygiene rules in GB, it is worth considering a recent amendment to this regulation that occurred after IP completion day.

Commission Regulation 2021/382 of 3 March 2021 amends the Annexes to Regulation 852/2004.

These amendments relate to requirements for food donation, allergen management and food safety culture (which follows on from food safety culture being adopted by Codex Alimentarius in its General Principles of Food Hygiene which was revised in September 2020).

Although now enacted in EU food law, the concept of a food safety culture is not unknown in the UK and incorporates management commitment with effective communication to identify and resolve food safety hazards and risks. It aims to change behaviour so that everyone in the food business does the right thing all the time and when nobody is watching. It instils a positive attitude into a food business and has many benefits for the business and for consumers.

Reference may be made to the Food Standards Agency's food safety culture toolkit, 2102, and its recent revision.

The concept of a food safety culture will feature more prominently as time goes by in GB and in the EU. It is based on a philosophy and a series of positive actions not just showing that there are written documents headed 'Food Safety Culture'.

Creating and maintaining a suitable food safety culture may assist the business to build a positive relationship with its regulator.

Hygiene of foodstuffs – the general rules – Regulation 852/2004

Food hygiene rules are intended to ensure a high level of consumer protection with regard to food safety in three main ways:

1. Legislation to prescribe minimum hygiene standards;

2. Effective official controls to check levels of compliance by food business operators; and

3. The creation, operation and maintenance of appropriate food safety management systems and procedures based on HACCP principles (Hazard Analysis and Critical Control Point).

(See for example, Recitals 7 and 12).

In addition to the Recitals, from the practitioner's perspective there are three key, but interrelated, parts to the Regulation:

1. Chapter 1 – the general provisions;

2. Chapter 2 – food business operators' obligations; and

3. The Annexes

Regulation 852/2004 imposes the following main obligations:

1. Primary responsibility for compliance rests with the FBO (Article 1 (1) (a) and Article 3);

2. The Regulation applies without prejudice to more specific requirements relating to food hygiene (Article 1);

3. The FBO must "ensure that at all stages of production, processing and distribution of food under their control satisfy the relevant hygiene requirements laid down in this Regulation" – obligations from "farm to fork" or "from conception to consumption" (Article 3);

4. FBOs carrying out primary production and associated operations must comply with the general requirements of Annex I (Article 4 (1)) and any specific rules in Regulation 853/2004;

5. FBOs carrying out any stage of production, processing and distribution of food after primary production and associated

operations must comply with the general requirements of Annex II (Article 4 (2)) and any specific rules in Regulation 853/2004;

6. As appropriate, FBOs must adopt specific hygiene measures (Article 4 (3));

   a) Compliance with microbiological criteria for foodstuffs (see above – Regulation 2073/2005),

   b) Procedures necessary to meet targets set to achieve the objectives of this Regulation,

   c) Compliance with temperature control for foodstuffs (e.g. cooking and reheating),

   d) Maintenance of the cold chain, and

   e) Sampling and analysis

7. FBOs must put in place, implement and maintain a permanent procedure or procedures based on the HACCP principles (Article 5);

8. FBOs must cooperate with the competent authorities and notify them of each establishment under their control or, where required, obtain approval for the food business.

   Article 6 (1) of the retained EU law states; "Food business operators shall cooperate with the competent authorities in accordance with the legislation in force in the relevant constituent territory of Great Britain."

The following is a selection of some of the main points arising in practice from the provisions of Regulation 852/2004.

<u>Chapter 1 – General provisions (Articles 1 and 2)</u>

Regulation 852/2004 does not generally apply to:

1. Food prepared for private domestic consumption (Article 1 (2) (a) and (b)); and

2. To the direct supply, by the producer, of small quantities of primary products to the final consumer or to local retail establishments directly supplying the final consumer. This is not defined in Regulation 852/2004 and it is left to the appropriate authority (which replaces the words "Member States" in the EU version of the Regulation) to establish rules which "achieve the objectives of this Regulation" (Article 1 (3)). (see for example, the FSA's guidance on the approval of food establishments referred to below as part of the discussion of Regulation 853/2004))

   The appropriate authority is defined in Article 2 of regulation 852/2004 in a way that is common to much retained EU legislation (England, the Secretary of State; Wales, the Welsh Ministers; Scotland, the Scottish Ministers)

Food hygiene, hereinafter called 'hygiene', means the measures and conditions necessary to control hazards and to ensure fitness for human consumption of a foodstuff taking into account its intended use (Article 2 (a)).

<u>Chapter II – Food business operators' obligations – HACCP</u>

Article 5 (1) states; "Food business operators shall put in place, implement and maintain a permanent procedure or procedures based on the HACCP principles."

The procedure must be business-specific. What might be a suitable system for a large retailer may not be the same for a small bakery, and an "off the shelf" generic food safety management system is unlikely to meet the FBO's needs or satisfy the competent authority, or indeed be sufficient to protect consumers.

The system need not be over complicated and, as it has to be understood and implemented by staff within the business, there is an argument for saying the simpler the better! A flow chart of key stages and actions is often a useful way of presenting the system.

Some FBOs may decide that they do not need to engage an external food safety consultant.

There is plenty of guidance available to help food businesses up and maintain a food safety management system and some competent authorities offer free training to FBOs. This is a very useful resource which if not utilised may be relevant when an FBO is being sentenced for a food offence.

The following general points about the food safety management system/HACCP may be made here (and note the relationship with the requirements of a positive food safety culture referred to above):

1. Lead from the top. An obvious point but unless the FBO and senior staff show commitment to achieve good, or best, practice it can be difficult to implement consistently high standards at every level of the organisation. The FBO must understand that they are operating a *food* business not just any old business;

2. Money alone will not create and operate a thriving, robust and suitable system;

3. Make sure the organisation is following the basic procedures of good hygiene such as cleaning, personal hygiene, training, pest control, operating in suitable premises and using suitable equipment, and zoning to prevent cross-contamination;

4. Communicate with staff. Tell them about HACCP, explain what it means, why it is important, the consequences of things going wrong and how each member of staff plays an important role in the process. As with all procedures, HACCP will not and cannot work unless management provides adequate support, not just financial, and staff feel valued and they "buy in" to its ethos (this means management must identify and communicate the ethos and creating a positive food safety culture);

5. Create a HACCP team. The size of the organisation and the type of activities undertaken will determine the composition of the team

but one or more committed staff members must "take ownership" of the HACCP system;

6. Review each stage of the FBO's activities and identify the hazards to see what could go wrong; intake of goods at the wrong temperature, incorrect handling or storage of products, cooking and cooling, display of foods in a serve over counter or a fridge at the wrong temperature;

7. Critical Control Point (CCP) relates to controlling hazards. An obvious one might be to cook food at the right temperature for the correct length of time;

8. Critical limits – to check that the CCP is working by specifying the actual temperature and length of time of the cooking process that will kill pathogens such as *E.coli* 157;

9. Monitor how the CCP is being controlled and record events such as cooking or the temperature of a food in a refrigerator or hot holding facility;

10. Corrective actions to be taken when the monitoring process indicates that a CCP is not under control. If a product has been outside the "safe" temperature for a period of time, what should happen to the product? Can it be used safely or should it be discarded?

11. Verify the system in action to check it is working effectively and if not make changes, record them and retrain staff as appropriate;

12. Suitable documentation and records must be maintained, kept up to date and checked by supervisors and management. If they indicate a potential problem this should be investigated. Supervisors should also make random checks of the matters being recorded (i.e. actually check the temperature of the food and not just record the temperature of the equipment or storage unit). Don't always rely on what is written on the document; it may not be accurate.

The Annexes

Although the legislation tells FBOs what to achieve it leaves them to find the most suitable way of achieving this within their own business.

This can be seen in the use of words such as "where necessary"; "where appropriate"; "adequate" and "sufficient" which are interpreted in a way that achieves the objectives of the Regulation (Article 2 (3)).

The Annexes set out the rules applicable to FBOs involved in primary production and associated operations in relation to animals, plants, fish and game (Annex I) and FBOs involved at stages after primary production (Annex II).

Annex I includes requirements to protect food from contamination, keep facilities clean, for training staff on health risks, cleanliness of animals going to slaughter and record-keeping.

Annex II covers a number of specific topics including the cleanliness and structure of the premises, marquees, market stalls, vans, transporting food, keeping articles and equipment which come into contact with food clean and disinfected, handling food waste, personal hygiene and staff illness, protecting foods from contamination, controlling pests and training.

By way of example, reference may be made to the following.

Annex II, Chapter I, paragraph 4 states:

> *"An adequate number of washbasins is to be available, suitably located and designated for cleaning hands. Washbasins for cleaning hands are to be provided with hot and cold running water, materials for cleaning hands and for hygienic drying. Where necessary, the facilities for washing food are to be separate from the hand-washing facility."*

This provision was the subject of a reference for a preliminary ruling to the Court of Justice of the European Union under Article 267 of the TFEU by the Austrian Courts in a case concerning a public house which served "almost no food, except toast". The washing facility in the premises was equipped with hot running water which could be used for washing hands but was also used for washing dishes.

The Court of Justice made the following remarks:

1. A wash basin for the purposes of paragraph 4 does not mean one that must be used exclusively for washing hands;

2. The final sentence of paragraph 4 makes clear that the same basin may be used for washing hands and for washing food, otherwise there would be no need to require that, where necessary, hands and food must be washed in separate equipment;

3. As the phrase "where necessary" must be read having regard to the objectives of the rules, it is not necessary to have a washing facility exclusively for washing hands where there is a facility for washing food (it all depends on the circumstances, the hazards and the risks and what steps are needed to protect consumers).

See *Astrid Preissl KEG v Landeshauptmann von Wien* (Case C-381/10).

Another case heard by the Court of Justice is also instructive as to the approach to interpreting and applying the food hygiene legislation.

In *Albrecht and others v Landeshauptmann von Wien* (Case C- 382/10).

The applicable provision in that case was Annex II, Chapter IX, paragraph 3;

> *"At all stages of production, processing and distribution, food is to be protected against any contamination likely to render the food unfit for human consumption, injurious to health or contaminated in such a way that it would be unreasonable to expect it to be consumed in that state."*

1. The Austrian authorities directed traders to install containers for the self-service supply of bread and bakery products so they could only be removed using technical means such as tongs, and once items had been removed, they could not be replaced;

2. The risk identified by the authorities was that the containers, which were already in use in Germany without undue cause for concern, allowed customers to touch and remove the products by hand, or cough or sneeze on them and could replace product which they had already removed. These activities could cause germs to be deposited on the products;

3. The authorities did not present evidence of actual contamination of the products;

4. Experts in Germany and Austria opined that the use of the containers did not create hygiene problems and as such it was reasonable for the traders to have regard to this when selecting the containers for use;

5. In all the circumstances the Court stated that:

    - it cannot be concluded that food business operators have infringed paragraph 3 on the basis only of the finding that a potential purchaser could conceivably have touched the foodstuffs by hand or sneezed on them;

    - it was necessary to consider the food safety management system implemented by the traders under Article 5 (to prevent, eliminate or reduce to acceptable levels the hazards); and

    - the authorities must determine that the food safety management system was insufficient in the light of all the available relevant information.

The mere presence of a risk that someone might sneeze on the bread, which might cause contamination, and might replace the bread was, on the facts of the case, insufficient to show a breach of chapter IX, paragraph 3.

These principles remain applicable in GB when interpreting the hygiene legislation.

Hygiene of foodstuffs – laying down specific hygiene rules for food of animal origin Regulation 853/2004

Article 1 (1) of Regulation 853/2004 states that the Regulation, "lays down specific rules on the hygiene of food of animal origin for food business operators. These rules supplement those laid down by Regulation 852/2004. They shall apply to unprocessed and processed products of animal origin."

General non-application of Regulation 853/2004

The Regulation does not apply to:

a) primary production for private domestic use;

b) the domestic preparation, handling or storage of food for private domestic consumption;

c) the direct supply, by the producer, of small quantities of primary products to the final consumer or to local retail establishments directly supplying the final consumer;

d) the direct supply, by the producer, of small quantities of meat from poultry and lagomorphs slaughtered on the farm to the final consumer or to local retail establishments directly supplying such meat to the final consumer as fresh meat;

e) hunters who supply small quantities of wild game or wild game meat directly to the final consumer or to local retail establishments directly supplying the final consumer; and

f) retail (although there are particular rules applying to retail that must be examined on a case-by-case basis – see for example Article 1(5))

Rules governing the activities referred to in paragraphs (c), (d) and (e) are set by the appropriate authority (as defined above) (Article 1 (4)).

Guidance on the application of the various exemption criteria can be found in FSA publications such as its Operational Policy for the Approval of Establishments.

Definitions for the purposes of Regulation 853

For the purposes of this Regulation, Annex I contains important definitions including; meat, live bivalve molluscs, fishery products, milk, eggs, frogs' legs and snails.

'Products of animal origin' means: food of animal origin, including honey and blood; live bivalve molluscs, live echinoderms, live tunicates and live marine gastropods intended for human consumption; and other animals destined to be prepared with a view to being supplied live to the final consumer.

Under the heading "meat" in Annex I, are definitions of "mechanically separated meat" (paragraph 1.14) and "meat preparations" (paragraph 1.15). These seemingly innocuous terms have been the subject of a long series of cases before the English Courts and a reference to the Court of Justice of the European Union (*R (on the application of Newby Foods Limited) v Food Standards Agency [2019] UKSC 18* and the decision of the CJEU *(C-453/13)*).

Some other aspects of Regulation 853/2004

Premises/establishments

Only products prepared and handled exclusively in establishments that meet the applicable requirements of food law and have been registered or, where required, approved by the competent authority may be placed on the market (Article 4).

With certain exceptions, establishments handling products of animal origin for which Annex III lays down specific requirements (e.g. transporting and slaughtering animals) require approval by the relevant competent authority before they can operate.

Annex III covers products of animal origin including: meat from various animals (cattle, pigs, poultry, lagomorphs and game); minced meat, meat preparations, meat products and mechanically separated meat; fish, milk, eggs and frogs' legs and snails. It sets out, in many respects quite detailed, requirements covering many aspects of production of these products such as the layout of premises), hygiene matters, compositional requirements and labelling.

Product marking

Product of animal origin may only be placed on the market if it has been handled in an establishment subject to approval and it has either:

(a) a health mark applied in accordance with Regulation (EC) No 854/2004 (now see Article 18 of regulation 2017/625 on official controls);

or

(b) when that Regulation does not provide for the application of a health mark, an identification mark applied in accordance with Annex II, Section I, of this Regulation

Since 1 January 2021, there are different requirements for marking depending on the geographical location of the approved establishment and the identity of the approving authority. The mark will still be an oval shape but will contain, United Kingdom, UK or GB followed by the approval number for FSA approved premises in GB and United Kingdom (Northern Ireland) or UK (NI) for FSA approved premises in NI. Similar provisions apply to local authority approved establishments.

It should be noted that there are additional specific labelling requirements for products such as beef.

Products of animal origin from outside Great Britain

Article 6 of Regulation 853/2004 prescribes that; "Food business operators importing products of animal origin from third countries shall ensure that importation takes place only if" certain criteria are met.

These include the country of dispatch and the establishment form where the product was dispatched are on approved lists, the products comply with all hygiene and related laws and the appropriate certificates and other documents are provided.

Practical application – enforcement action under the hygiene regulations

Enforcement action for non-compliance with the hygiene rules might result in the service of an enforcement notice and/or a criminal prosecution.

The FBO's response to either or both of these events depends on a careful assessment of the situation; is the enforcement officer's opinion of the circumstances justified, reasonable and supported by cogent and admissible evidence; what is the impact of the action on the food business; can steps be taken to minimise the impact of the action (e.g. carry out a deep clean and re-open the business within a day or two); what are the cost and other resource implications of compliance and/or challenging the action.

It is very important that the official's factual assessment of the conditions in the food business is reviewed in light of the purpose and objective of food hygiene legislation.

It might be very difficult to argue that a photograph showing raw meat placed directly above ready to eat salad with the consequential dripping of meat juice onto the salad, or evidence of ready to eats foods being prepared on a chopping board also being used for raw meat are anything other than a contravention (see for example Regulation 852/2004, Annex II, Chapter IX, paragraph 3). There is a hazard which leads to a risk.

However, cracked floor tiles in a restaurant may not be capable of being effectively cleaned and should be placed or repaired but, depending on the circumstances, the effect of this defect *may* not be sufficient to amount to a breach requiring enforcement action, having regard to the purpose and objective of the legislation (see for example Regulation 852/2004 Annex II, Chapter 1, paragraph 1). There may be a hazard, but does it lead to a risk?

There may be a difference between action that *should* be taken to make good minor deficiencies as a matter of good practice and those steps which *must* be taken to remedy a legal contravention. The two can become blurred and competent authorities must ensure the distinction is maintained, particularly in an inspection report or enforcement notice requiring the FBO to take action.

The FBO should also be clear about which requirements are required by law and which might be based on good practice. Where appropriate, the latter might be the subject of a challenge.

All circumstances are different and each situation must be looked individually having regard, as appropriate, to first principles including the identification of a hazard and then assessing the risk consequential on that hazard.

Conclusion

Operating a compliant food business depends on having proper food safety management systems in place and following all applicable hygiene rules.

The basic rules of good hygiene remain the same and although staff can be trained to undertake certain responsibilities, they need to be made to feel part of a team. They need to appreciate that what they do and don't do has an impact on their colleagues and ultimately the business as a whole.

Developing and maintaining a positive food safety culture alongside solid and robust food safety management systems will go a long way to creating the foundations for a compliant and successful business.

CHAPTER FIVE

FOOD INFORMATION TO CONSUMERS

Introduction

Providing consumers with sufficient information to allow them to make informed choices about the food they eat is one of the main pillars of food law.

This information may be provided on the product label, on a restaurant menu, on a website or in other advertising or marketing material.

These information rules may be divided into general rules contained in Regulation (EU) No 1169/2011 on the provision of food information to consumers (which will be the focus of this chapter and referred to as FIC) and additional rules specific to a food or food type (e.g. chocolate or food supplements).

This information may be required to keep consumers safe (warning them about substances causing allergies – peanuts for example) or to allow them to make personal choices (following a vegetarian or vegan diet) or for environmental benefits (eco-labelling).

The provision of food information is also relevant to developments in policy which may affect the food itself (e.g. compositional changes to reduce salt, sugar, fat etc.) or the way in which information is provided (e.g. traffic lights to denote levels of salt, sugar, fat etc.) or environmental considerations (e.g. the carbon footprint of the food and its method of production).

Food business operators (FBOs) may make statements or claims about their products for example, "natural", "pure" or "fresh". When advising on compliance it may be necessary to have regard to guidance issued by the competent authorities and others, case law and also rulings of the Advertising Standards Authority.

There are many rules and requirements that touch on food information and labelling that it is impossible to include them all. This chapter will therefore review the main provisions of FIC and refer briefly to some other labelling rules.

Retained EU law and 'EU Exit' Regulations

Retained EU law

Regulation 1169/2011

Domestic law

The Food Information Regulations 2014, as amended (and similar regulations in Wales and Scotland)

EU Exit Regulations

The Food (Amendment) (EU Exit) Regulations 2020 (2020 No. 1501)

The Food and Drink (Amendment) (EU Exit) Regulations 2020 (2020 No. 1627)

The Food and Drink (Miscellaneous Amendments Relating to Food and Wine Composition, Information and Labelling) Regulations 2021 (2021 No. 632)

Allergens and PPDS – a recent UK development

Friday, 1 October 2021 saw a significant domestic development in the provision of food safety information. Since then, foods that are prepacked for direct sale (PPDS) are required to provide a full ingredients list which emphasises the name of the allergenic ingredient (see below discussion on the labelling of allergens in respect of prepacked foods).

This change in the law, dubbed "Natasha's Law" after Natasha Ednan-Laperouse who died after eating a pre-packaged baguette containing sesame to which she was allergic. At the time the baguette was not required to contain ingredients labelling.

Food that is packaged at the same place it is offered or sold to consumers and is in this packaging before it is ordered or selected is PPDS. This might be sandwiches that are packed on site before the customer orders them or a burger in packaging kept hot pending sale.

Reference should be made to guidance issued by the Food Standards Agency, Food Standards Scotland and other organisations.

This law was introduced by an amendment to the Food Information Regulations:

The Food Information (Amendment) (England) Regulations 2019;

The Food Information (Wales) (Amendment) (No. 2) Regulations 2020;

The Food Information (Amendment No. 2) Regulations (Northern Ireland) 2020 and

The Food Information (Scotland) Amendment Regulations 2021

The Provision of Food Information to Consumers Regulation 1169/2011 (FIC)

The provision of food information shall pursue a high level of protection of consumers' health and interests by providing a basis for final consumers to make informed choices and to make safe use of food, with particular regard to health, economic, environmental, social and ethical considerations (Article 3 (1)).

Any food intended for supply to the final consumer or to mass caterers must be accompanied by food information in accordance with FIC (Article 6).

Selected definitions – Article 2

The definitions contained in other retained EU law (such as Regulations 178/2002, 852/2004 and 853/2004) apply for the purposes of Regulation 1169/2011.

Food information

Information concerning a food and made available to the final consumer by means of a label, other accompanying material, or any other means including modern technology tools or verbal communication.

Food information law

The EU-derived domestic legislation or retained direct EU legislation governing the food information, and in particular labelling, including rules of a general nature applicable to all foods in particular circumstances or to certain categories of foods and rules which apply only to specific foods.

Mandatory food information

The particulars that are required to be provided to the final consumer by EU-derived domestic legislation or retained direct EU legislation.

Prepacked food

Any single item for presentation as such to the final consumer and to mass caterers, consisting of a food and the packaging into which it was put before being offered for sale, whether such packaging encloses the food completely or only partially, but in any event in such a way that the contents cannot be altered without opening or changing the packaging.

Mass caterer

Any establishment (including a vehicle or a fixed or mobile stall), such as restaurants, canteens, schools, hospitals and catering enterprises in which, in the course of a business, food is prepared to be ready for consumption by the final consumer.

Ingredient

Any substance or product, including flavourings, food additives and food enzymes, and any constituent of a compound ingredient, used in the manufacture or preparation of a food and still present in the finished product, even if in an altered form; residues shall not be considered as 'ingredients'

Labelling

Any words, particulars, trademarks, brand name, pictorial matter or symbol relating to a food and placed on any packaging, document, notice, label, ring or collar accompanying or referring to such food.

Article 7 sets out some general principles under the heading of "Fair Information Practices" and provides that food information:

- must not be misleading;
- must be accurate, clear and easy to understand for the consumer;
- must not attribute the property of preventing, treating or curing a human disease, nor refer to such properties

Those prohibitions also apply to advertising and to the general way in which foods are presented (e.g. shape, appearance or packaging).

When considering the presentation of foods, reference should also be made to Article 16 of Regulation 178/2002.

Responsibilities for food information – Article 8

Article 8 sets out detailed provisions for establishing who is responsible for providing food information along the food chain.

Article 8 (1) in the retained EU law now states:

> "The food business operator responsible for the food information shall be the operator under whose name or business name the food

is marketed or, if that operator is not established in the British Islands, the importer into the British Islands."

The words "British Islands" was inserted by the Food and Drink (Miscellaneous Amendments Relating to Food and Wine Composition, Information and Labelling) Regulations 2021 and replace "Union" and "Union market" which appear in the EU version of Regulation 1169/2011.

The term "British Islands" is defined in the Interpretation Act 1978 as "the United Kingdom, the Channel Islands and the Isle of Man".

Some FBOs, such as retailers, simply buy and sell foodstuffs without doing anything to affect food information. FBOs are deemed to know the rules and must not supply foods which they know or presume, on the basis of information in their possession, to be non-compliant.

Within their businesses, FBOs must not modify food information if this would mislead the final consumer, reduce the level of consumer protection or impede the making of consumer choices. This might apply to extending 'use-by' dates on bulk product (e.g. ham) that the FBO retailer opens and cuts up for sale to consumers (e.g. for sandwiches).

Each FBO must provide proper food information to the next FBO in line so when food is supplied to the final consumer it is properly labelled (maintaining the integrity of the "information chain").

A break in the information chain could create a safety issue for consumers with allergies and could significantly mislead consumers requiring particular types of food including vegetarians and vegans.

Mandatory food information – Article 9 and 10

Articles 9 and 10 of FIC set out the mandatory food information required for prepacked food.

The mandatory particulars as set out in Article 9 (1):

(a) the name of the food;

(b) the list of ingredients;

(c) any ingredient or processing aid listed in Annex II or derived from a substance or product listed in Annex II causing allergies or intolerances used in the manufacture or preparation of a food and still present in the finished product, even if in an altered form;

(d) the quantity of certain ingredients or categories of ingredients (QUID);

(e) the net quantity of the food;

(f) the date of minimum durability or the 'use by' date;

(g) any special storage conditions and/or conditions of use;

(h) the name or business name and address of the food business operator referred to in Article 8(1);

(i) the country of origin or place of provenance where provided for in Article 26;

(j) instructions for use where it would be difficult to make appropriate use of the food in the absence of such instructions;

(k) with respect to beverages containing more than 1,2 % by volume of alcohol, the actual alcoholic strength by volume;

(l) a nutrition declaration.

Although Article 9 contains a list of mandatory food information, it is supplemented by additional requirements in Article 10 and detailed rules in other parts of FIC (e.g. Articles 12 – 35 and the Annexes).

It is not possible to review each of the requirements but the following contains references to allergens, date of minimum durability, country of origin and place of provenance and the mandatory nutrition declaration.

Ingredients causing allergies or intolerances (Article 9 (1) (c))

Substances causing allergies or intolerances are relevant to four main topics:

1) Hygiene law – preventing inadvertent cross-contamination;

2) General food law – placing unsafe food on the market;

3) General criminal law – prosecutions, including the offence of manslaughter (see *R v Mohammed Khalique Zaman* [2017] EWCA Crim 1783 by way of example); and

4) Food information law – warning consumers about the presence of those substances which are actually used in the manufacture or production of the food and which are still present in the final product.

Food information law requirements to highlight allergens applies when the substance is used as an ingredient in a food. Where it might be contained in the final product due to potential cross-contamination, a "may contain" warning might be required (see below).

There are 14 "substances or products causing allergies or intolerances" set out in Annex II to EUFIC. Food information law only applies to these 14 substances or products even though some people may have adverse reactions to other foodstuffs (for example strawberries or kiwi fruit).

The 14 are:

1. Cereals containing gluten, namely: wheat (such as spelt and khorasan wheat), rye, barley, oats or their hybridised strains, and products thereof;

2. Crustaceans and products thereof;

3. Eggs and products thereof;

4. Fish and products thereof;

5. Peanuts and products thereof;

6. Soybeans and products thereof:

7. Milk and products thereof (including lactose);

8. Nuts, namely: almonds (Amygdalus communis L.), hazelnuts (Corylus avellana), walnuts (Juglans regia), cashews (Anacardium occidentale), pecan nuts (Carya illinoinensis (Wangenh.) K. Koch), Brazil nuts (Bertholletia excelsa), pistachio nuts (Pistacia vera), macadamia or Queensland nuts (Macadamia ternifolia), and products thereof, except for nuts used for making alcoholic distillates including ethyl alcohol of agricultural origin;

9. Celery and products thereof;

10. Mustard and products thereof;

11. Sesame seeds and products thereof;

12. Sulphur dioxide and sulphites at concentrations of more than 10 mg/kg or 10 mg/litre in terms of the total SO2 which are to be calculated for products as proposed ready for consumption or as reconstituted according to the instructions of the manufacturers;

13. Lupin and products thereof;

14. Molluscs and products thereof.

Allergens – prepacked foods – Article 21

Any of the above ingredients present in the final food must be listed within the list of ingredients "with a clear reference to the name of the substance or product" which must be "emphasised through a typeset that clearly distinguishes it from the rest of the list of ingredients, for example by means of the font, style or background colour."

This is usually indicated by a statement on the label adjacent to the list of ingredients, "for allergens see ingredients in …" followed by in bold, red or however the FBO has chosen to highlight the allergen ingredient.

When developing the label, it is important to see how this actually looks in practice to ensure that the particular substance "stands out from the other ingredients". Care should be taken to ensure that what appears on the computer screen as very clearly highlighting the allergen is replicated as clearly on the actual packaging. The quality of the printing, typeset and clarity of colours on the final label may have an impact on this.

Where the food does not require a list of ingredients (see Article 19) the information is provided by using the word "contains" followed by the correct name of the allergenic ingredient; for example, a wine label would state; "Contains – Sulphites".

The ingredient should be highlighted using the correct terminology. The description, "wheat" (or the other cereal by name) should be used rather than "gluten" and "milk" rather than "dairy".

Precautionary statements – "may contain" – risk of inadvertent cross-contamination

Although one or more of the 14 substances may not have been used as an ingredient in a foodstuff it may have been made in premises that handle one or more of them. If there is a real chance that the final product might inadvertently contain one or more of the 14 due to inadvertent cross-contamination, the label or information could refer to "may contain" followed by the name of the ingredient. This should only be done following a proper risk assessment rather than simply as means of protecting the FBO.

It is arguably not good practice to label a food with a statement such as, this product might contain all 14 allergens (i.e. list all of them on the label) or this product contains a number of the substances (listed by name) in Annex II. This might indicate that the business does not really know what is in its food and therefore consumers might find it difficult to have trust in other statements and claims made about the product.

Awareness of problems with allergens

Providing allergen information can be challenging, particularly in sectors such as hospitality, and requires all staff to be fully trained in relation to the 14 substances and how these are used in the final food. Great care must be taken to update the allergen information when introducing new foods to the menu, developing existing recipes or changing suppliers.

Due to the serious implications of susceptible consumers eating food which contains these substances, some FBOs are training staff in how to identify and respond to consumers who have adverse reactions.

Date of minimum durability and use by date (Article 9 (1) (f))

A "date of minimum durability" (a best before date) is an indication of the timeframe within which the food retains its optimum qualities. Beyond this date food will deteriorate and may not taste as fresh, but may still be safe to eat.

This date is replaced by a "use by" date where from, a microbiological point of view, foods are highly perishable and are therefore likely after a short period to constitute an immediate danger to human health" (Article 24).

As the use by date concerns safety, food should not be consumed once the use by date has expired. This is highly relevant to general food law issues in that Article 24 states, "after the 'use by' date a food shall be deemed to be unsafe in accordance with Article 14(2) to (5) of Regulation (EC) No 178/2002".

This imposes stringent obligations on FBOs to have a clear, robust and functioning system around stock rotation and was the subject of a 2021 court case involving Tesco and the display of food past its use by date in which the District Judge imposed a fine in excess of £7.5 million (see chapter 10 on sentencing).

The correct use of date marking and the correct understanding of its meaning by consumers help to play a big part in reducing food waste.

Country of origin and place of provenance (Article 9 (1) (i))

Mandatory food information requires "the country of origin or place of provenance where provided for in Article 26".

Article 26 states that an indication of the country of origin or place of provenance is mandatory for specified meat and also;

> "where failure to indicate this might mislead the consumer as to the true country of origin or place of provenance of the food, in particular if the information accompanying the food or the label as a whole would otherwise imply that the food has a different country of origin or place of provenance".

This might apply where a label indicates that the food comes from a certain country, perhaps by using an image of the country's flag, but the food is made elsewhere.

There are also requirements where the country of origin or the place of provenance of a food is given and where it is not the same as that of its primary ingredient which means;

> "an ingredient or ingredients of a food that represent more than 50 % of that food or which are usually associated with the name of the food by the consumer and for which in most cases a quantitative indication is required" (Article 2 of Regulation 1169/2011).

Country of origin and place of provenance are defined and provide a useful example of the legislative changes required since IP completion day (words changed are in bold).

Country of origin in the EU version of regulation 1169/2011:

> "For the purposes of this Regulation the country of origin of a food shall refer to the origin of a food as determined in accordance with **Articles 23 to 26 of Regulation (EEC) No 2913/92.**" (now the Union Customs Code)

Whereas, in the GB retained EU law it has become:

> "For the purposes of this Regulation the country of origin of a food shall refer to the origin of a food as determined in accordance with **section 17(2) to (4) of the Taxation (Cross-border Trade) Act 2018, as read with the Customs (Origin**

> **of Chargeable Goods) (EU Exit) Regulations 2020, insofar as those subsections and Regulations relate to the determination of the country of origin of a food.**"

Place of provenance in the EU version of regulation 1169/2011:

> 'place of provenance' means any place where a food is indicated to come from, and that is not the 'country of origin' as determined in accordance with **Articles 23 to 26 of Regulation (EEC) No 2913/92** (again now a reference to the Union Customs Code); the name, business name or address of the food business operator on the label shall not constitute an indication of the country of origin or place of provenance of food within the meaning of this Regulation;

In the GB retained EU law it has become:

> "'place of provenance' means any place where a food is indicated to come from, and that is not the 'country of origin' as determined in accordance with **section 17(2) to (4) of the Taxation (Cross-border Trade) Act 2018, as read with the Customs (Origin of Chargeable Goods) (EU Exit) Regulations 2020, insofar as those subsections and Regulations relate to the determination of the country of origin of a food**; the name, business name or address of the food business operator on the label shall not constitute an indication of the country of origin or place of provenance of food within the meaning of this Regulation;"

For a discussion of the meaning of country of origin and place of provenance reference may be made to the Judgment of the Court of Justice in *Organisation juive europeenne v Ministre de l'Economie et des Finances Case C-363/18* (foodstuffs originating in the territories occupied by the State of Israel).

Mandatory nutrition information – Article 9 (1) (l)

Section 3 of FIC provides detailed information about how this information is provided. This does not apply to food supplements and natural mineral waters which are governed by their own GB regulations which are listed in Article 29.

The following is a note of some, but not all, of the general requirements relating to mandatory nutrition information (see Annex V for foods that are exempt from this requirement).

The mandatory nutrition declaration *must* include (Article 30 (1)) – often referred to as "back of pack":

> The energy value;
>
> And the amounts of -
>
> fat; saturates; carbohydrate; sugars; protein and salt

The FBO may choose to repeat that information and this is often referred to as "front of pack" information (Article 30 (3)). The FBO may only repeat information by stating:

> The energy value, or
>
> The energy value together with the amounts of fat, saturates, sugars and salt.

Article 30 (2) states that the mandatory nutrition declaration *may* be supplemented by providing the amounts of one or more of:

> Mono-unsaturates; Polyunsaturates; Polyols; Starch; Fibre; any of the vitamins or minerals in compliance with the rules in Annex XIII of EUFIC (including vitamins such as A and C and minerals such as calcium and potassium).

The rules provide for how this information is to be provided.

Other aspects of the rules concern: non-prepacked food (Articles 30 (5) and 44); how to calculate the values for the ingredients (Articles 30 (1), 30 (5) and 31 (3)) and how to display information (e.g. per 100 g/100 ml and per portion – Articles 32 and 33) and the method of presentation (Article 34).

As well as FBOs checking the accuracy of their information, competent authorities may take samples to check composition levels against the values stated on pack. It is therefore important that the FBO can readily and easily substantiate and support the amounts declared on pack and provide that information to the authority if required.

Additional mandatory particulars – Article 10 and Annex III

Mandatory information, the precise details of which are prescribed, must be given for the following:

- Foods packaged in certain gases to extend their durability;
- Foods containing sweeteners;
- Foods containing glycyrrhizinic acid (liquorice);
- Beverages with high caffeine content and foods with added caffeine;
- Foods with added phytosterols, phytosterol esters, phytostanols or phytostanol esters; and
- Frozen meat, frozen meat preparations and frozen unprocessed fishery products

Presentation of mandatory food information

Articles 12 and 13 prescribe how mandatory information is to be presented:

- It must be available and easily accessible for all foods;
- For prepacked foods it must appear directly on the package or on a label attached thereto;
- It must be marked in a conspicuous place in such a way as to be easily visible, clearly legible and, where appropriate, indelible. It

must not in any way be hidden, obscured, detracted from or interrupted by any other written or pictorial matter or any other intervening material;

- It must be of the appropriate font size (1.2 mm or 0.9 mm)
- The name of the food, the net quantity and, where appropriate, the actual alcoholic strength by volume must appear in the same field of vision

Article 14 sets out rules applying to foods "offered by means of distance communication" including via the internet.

Article 15 in the retained EU law now states that mandatory food information "shall appear in English" but that "shall not preclude the particulars from being indicated in several languages".

This important because if certain information, for example about substances causing allergens, is not provided in English this may make the food unsafe which might require a product recall and lead to a regulatory investigation.

Omission of certain mandatory particulars – Article 16

Article 16 provides a list of products which do not require full mandatory particulars. These include certain glass bottles, small packages (largest surface having an area of less than 10 cm2); products containing more than 1.2% alcohol).

Voluntary food information – Articles 36 and 37

Where mandatory food information as referred to in Articles 9 and 10 is provided on a voluntary basis, it must comply with applicable provisions of FIC (Article 36).

Voluntary food information must not be misleading (see Article 7), ambiguous or confusing for consumers and it must be based on the relevant scientific data, where this is applicable (Article 36).

Voluntary food information shall not be displayed to the detriment of the space available for mandatory food information (Article 37).

The power to impose national measures – Article 39

The EU version of Article 39 allows the Member States to impose mandatory particulars in addition to those in Article 9 (1) and Article 10 on four specified grounds.

In the retained version of Regulation 1169/2011 applicable in GB, Article 39 (1) states specifies the types of regulations that may be made in respect of those grounds:

> "In addition to the mandatory particulars referred to in Article 9(1) and in Article 10, nothing in this Regulation prevents the appropriate authority from making type A or B regulations requiring additional mandatory particulars for specific types or categories of foods, justified on grounds of at least one of the following:
>
> (a) in the case of type A regulations, the protection of public health;
>
> (b) in the case of type A or B regulations, the protection of consumers;
>
> (c) in the case of type A or B regulations, the prevention of fraud;
>
> (d) in the case of type A regulations, the protection of industrial and commercial property rights, indications of provenance, registered designations of origin and the prevention of unfair competition."

The appropriate authority is defined in a new provision inserted into Article 2 (general definitions):

> (i) as regards type B regulations, the Secretary of State;
>
> (ii) in all other cases:

(aa) in relation to England, the Secretary of State;

(bb) in relation to Scotland, the Scottish Ministers;

(cc) in relation to Wales, the Welsh Ministers

The definitions of the types of regulations are also new additions to Article 2 and should be referred to in details but on a broad level:

Type A regulations made under the Food Safety Act 1990;

Type B regulations made under the Weights and Measures Act 1985;

Type C regulations made under provisions of regulation 1169/2011 listed in Annex 16 of the retained EU law (a new provision) which includes requirements applicable to QUID labelling and the mandatory nutrition declaration;

Type D regulations made under provisions of regulation 1169/2011 listed in Annex 17 of the retained EU law (another new provision) which includes the availability and placement of mandatory food information

Type E regulations made under Article 23 (2) (net quantity)

Non-prepacked food – Article 44

Article 44 of FIC relates to "National measures for non-prepacked food" and in the retained EU version states:

1. Where foods are offered for sale to the final consumer or to mass caterers without prepackaging, or where foods are packed on the sales premises at the consumer's request or prepacked for direct sale:

   (a) the provision of the particulars specified in point (c) of Article 9(1) is mandatory;

(b) the provision of the particulars specified in Articles 9(1)(e) is not mandatory but nothing in this Regulation prevents type B regulations from being made to make the provision of those particulars mandatory;

(c) the provision of the other particulars specified in Articles 9(1) and 10 is not mandatory but nothing in this Regulation prevents type A regulations from being made to make the provision of those particulars, or some of those particulars, mandatory.

2. Nothing in this Regulation prevents the appropriate authority from making type A or B regulations concerning the means through which the particulars or elements of those particulars specified in paragraph 1 are to be made available and, where appropriate, their form of expression and presentation.

Practical Application

Correctly classifying the food is crucial because without that information the FBO and their advisers do not know which regulatory scheme applies.

This point was highlighted above in connection with food supplements and medicinal products, but the point can be seen from the case of *The Queen on the application of Nutricia Limited and The Secretary of State for Health [2015] EWHC 2285 (Admin),* concerning whether or not a product could be "classified as a food for special medical purposes or "FSMP"".

At paragraph 22 of his judgment, Green J said:

> *"Under both EU and domestic law products intended to provide some form of nutritional supplementation to the human diet fall into four broad categories: fortified foods; food supplements; foods for particular nutritional uses (known as "PARNUTs"); and foods for special medical purposes ("FSMPs"). Each category is subject to a distinct regulatory framework."*

Information is conveyed to consumers by means of all the information on a product label and hence the use of words in a particular context may be important in establishing legal compliance.

The case of *Bundesverband der Verbraucherzentralen und Verbraucherverbände – Verbraucherzentrale Bundesverband eV v Teekanne GmbH and Co KG* (C-195/14) might be instructive to how these issues arise. The question arose as to whether or not a food label was misleading. Although the case was based on the previous general labelling regime contained in Directive 2000/13/EC, the general principles apply equally to EUFIC.

A food label contained images of raspberries and vanilla flowers and therefore a consumer might, perhaps reasonably, believe that they were contained in the product. The list of ingredients did not include references to these substances and hence, by omission, advised consumers that the product did not, in fact, contain them.

As consumers are expected to have regard to all the available information, the question arose as to whether the label was misleading in that the clear visual implication that the product contained raspberries and/or vanilla was only dispelled once the consumer carefully read the list of ingredients.

In its decision on a reference for a preliminary ruling from the German courts, the Court of Justice of the European Union advised that an accurate and complete list of ingredients might not be sufficient to correct the erroneous or misleading impression which the consumer gains from the labelling of the foodstuff.

Where the labelling of a foodstuff gives the impression that a particular ingredient is present in that foodstuff, even though it is not in fact present (this being apparent solely from the list of ingredients), the label could mislead the purchaser as to the characteristics of the foodstuff in question.

Whether the label is misleading depends on an assessment of the label as a whole and is a question of fact and law for the national courts to determine.

Due to the complex nature of food information and food labelling it is not always possible to provide definitive advice on the legality of a label or related marketing material having regard to food law. It is often possible to say that a phrase is not permissible, a red flag, (e.g. stating a food supplement will cure arthritis) or it is permissible, a green flag, (e.g. strictly following the legal requirement for example regarding the presentation of the mandatory nutrition declaration, or correctly using a nutrition or health claim).

Sometimes the advice might require an orange, or amber, flag. The proposed phrase or statement may be on the "cusp of compliance" and becoming compliant may require a, perhaps subtle, change of wording or emphasis or context, or it might depend on how others (competent authorities, consumers and commercial competitors) interpret the information conveyed.

Ultimately, where a label is challenged, and the parties cannot reach agreement on the application of the relevant rules, only a court can provide a definitive interpretation of the law in any given set of circumstances. Neither party may want matters to go that far.

Conclusion

Advising on labelling and food information is not always straightforward; there are many different rules to be taken into account.

Additionally, the adviser may need to be aware of potential "tensions", or competing interests, between the needs, requirements and desires of the FBO, the legal and compliance team and those involved in marketing and advertising. This may require a degree of compromise when finalising the information that will appear on the label.

There is clear scope for creativity and innovation in the development of food labels and other methods of communicating with consumers, but this is dependent on having an understanding of the basic rules and how they may be used legally to the FBOs advantage.

The EU aims to propose, by the end of 2022, new legislation on ways to harmonise front of pack labelling. This is part of the EU's Farm to Fork strategy. Stakeholders in GB will need to watch developments to see what impact, if any, this might have on GB food businesses selling into the EU.

Finally, one matter that is directly relevant to the UK's departure from the EU. The Food and Drink (miscellaneous Amendments Relating to Food and Wine Composition, Information and Labelling) Regulations 2021 inserted a new regulation 16 into the Food Information Regulations 2014.

The new regulation prohibits "an authorised officer of a food authority" may not serve an improvement notice on a person relating to a failure to comply with specified provisions of Regulation 1169/2011 such as the name or business name and address of the food business operator referred to in Article 8(1) where the improvement notice would relate to a specified product that was placed on the market on a date referrable to IP completion date and if on that date the labelling would have been compliant with FIC.

The detail in the regulation is important, but Regulation 16 is designed to give some leeway to making products compliant.

CHAPTER SIX

NUTRITION AND HEALTH CLAIMS

Introduction

Food business operators are keen to promote their products in most commercially advantageous way whilst remaining legally compliant.

One way of achieving this may be to emphasise the benefits of a food generally or specifically because of a substance that it contains or does not contain.

The making of nutrition and health claims is governed by Regulation (EC) No 1924/2006 on nutrition and health claims made on foods (NHCR).

Care must always be taken when making any claims to ensure that they are compliant with the relevant legislation and do not cross the line and make medicinal claims.

In general, compliant health claims refer to maintaining or supporting a healthy condition whereas claims referring to improving or curing a particular condition may be seen as medicinal.

As with other food-related subjects, there is plenty of guidance which is regularly updated. For example, on 10 November 2021 the UK Government updated its Nutrition and Health Claims Guidance (part of the Gov.UK Brexit Business Guidance).

Retained EU law and 'EU Exit' Regulations

Nutrition and Health Claims –

Retained law

Regulation 1924/2006

Domestic law

The Nutrition and Health Claims (England) Regulations 2007, as amended (and similar regulations for Wales and Scotland)

EU Exit Regulations

The Nutrition (Amendment etc.) (EU Exit) Regulations 2019 (2019 No. 651)

The Nutrition (Amendment etc.) (EU Exit) Regulations 2020 (2020 No. 1476)

Authorisations in GB since 1 January 2021

Prior to IP completion day, the authorisation of nutrition and health claims was made at EU level. Proposed health claims were reviewed by EFSA and a scientific opinion was prepared. When searching for information about whether a health claim was authorised and if so whether its use was subject to conditions, initial reference could be made to the EU register of nutrition and health claims made on foods and then checking this against the actual legislation that authorised the claim.

Regulation 1924/2006 remains valid in GB as retained EU law (i.e. the version that was in force on IP completion day). The main provisions regarding they definition of nutrition and health claims, how they may be used and additional labelling requirements are set out in that regulation.

The EU approach still applies to authorisations for products being placed on the market in the EU27 and in Northern Ireland but no longer in GB.

The above EU Exit regulations transferred responsibility for risk assessments and the like to GB authorities. Those regulations also made necessary provisions for the application process, the scientific evaluation of applications and the factors to be consider when a risks management decision is taken.

Since 1 January 2021 only nutrition and health claims that are authorised and are listed on the Great Britain Nutrition and Health Claims register (the NHC register which is in the form of an excel spreadsheet) may be used on the GB market. This is the GB equivalent of the EU Register of Nutrition and Health claims mentioned above.

The GB NHC register is required by virtue of Article 20 of the NHCR.

It is therefore necessary to review the GB and the EU registers if advising clients in GB and in the EU (including NI).

Claims that were authorised for use in the EU prior to 1 January 2021 appear on the GB NHC register. Vitamin C may be used as an example:

In the EU register which references Commission Regulation 432/2012 and the reference for the EFSA scientific opinion, the following authorised health claim appears

> "Vitamin C contributes to normal psychological function"

And the conditions of use are:

> "The claim may be used only for food which is at least a source of vitamin C as referred to in the claim SOURCE OF [NAME OF VITAMIN/S] AND/OR [NAME OF MINERAL/S] as listed in the Annex to Regulation (EC) No 1924/2006."

The same information appears on the GB NHC register along with the following words in column H of the register, "Authorised for use in Great Britain".

The GB NHC register also contains the list of authorised nutrition claims and the conditions of use that apply to them.

Full details of the GB application process can be found in various locations including the Gov.UK Nutrition Law website.

A GB Nutrition and Health Claims Committee has been set up to provide scientific advice to the UK government of the substantiation of scientific evidence in respect of applications. The Committee is supported by Public Health England.

UK Government advice is that applicants for health claims authorisation should submit a Medicines Borderline Advice Form to the Medicines and Healthcare products Regulatory Agency (MHRA). Whether this is done in any or every case is a matter for the applicant and its advisers.

Regulation 1924/2006 – general provisions

The NHCR contains rules governing claims generally and specifically to nutrition claims and to health claims.

As stated in Article 1, the Regulation applies to nutrition and health claims made in "commercial communications, whether in the labelling, presentation or advertising of foods to be delivered as such to the final consumer".

An issue that arises in practice is whether the making of the claim is in a "commercial communication", a term not defined in the NHCR.

Guidance on what is, and what is not a commercial communication can be found in Recital 4 of the NHCR which states that dietary guidelines or advice issued by public health authorities are communications that are not commercial in nature.

Further guidance may be found in a decision of the Court of Justice of the European Union, *Verband Sozialer Wettbewerb* (*Case C-19/15*) in which the Court had regard to other EU legislation in which the term commercial communication is defined and stated that in the context of the NHCR the term included a communication made in the form of advertising foods, designed to promote, directly or indirectly, those foods (see paragraph 29 of the Judgment).

The following definitions are taken from Article 2:

Claim

Means any message or representation, which is not mandatory under any enactment, including pictorial, graphic or symbolic representation, in any form, which states, suggests or implies that a food has particular characteristics.

Nutrition claim

Means any claim which states, suggests or implies that a food has particular beneficial nutritional properties due to:

(a) the energy (calorific value) it

(i) provides;

(ii) provides at a reduced or increased rate; or

(iii) does not provide; and/or

(b) the nutrients or other substances it

(i) contains;

(ii) contains in reduced or increased proportions; or

(iii) does not contain;

The claim must state, suggest or imply a *benefit* arising from the presence or absence of energy or nutrients.

Health claim

Means any claim that states, suggests or implies that a relationship exists between a food category, a food or one of its constituents and health

Article 2 also states that definitions in other food law legislation such as Regulation 178/2002 and Regulation 1169/2011 apply for the purposes of the NHCR.

Principles for all claims – Article 3

Article 3 now states:

Nutrition and health claims may be used in the labelling, presentation and advertising of foods placed on the market only if they comply with the provisions of this Regulation.

Without prejudice to Regulation (EU) No 1169/2011 and the Business Protection from Misleading Marketing Regulations 2008, the use of nutrition and health claims shall not:

(a) be false, ambiguous or misleading;

(b) give rise to doubt about the safety and/or the nutritional adequacy of other foods;

(c) encourage or condone excess consumption of a food;

(d) state, suggest or imply that a balanced and varied diet cannot provide appropriate quantities of nutrients in general. The appropriate authority may by regulations adopt derogations in the case of nutrients for which sufficient quantities cannot be provided by a balanced and varied diet, including the conditions for their application, taking into account the special conditions present in the parts of Great Britain in relation to which the regulations are to be made;

(e) refer to changes in bodily functions which could give rise to or exploit fear in the consumer, either textually or through pictorial, graphic or symbolic representations.

Nutrient profiles – Article 4

The appropriate authority may by regulations establish specific nutrient profiles, including exemptions, which food or certain categories of food must comply with in order to bear nutrition or health claims and the conditions for the use of nutrition or health claims for foods or categories of foods with respect to the nutrient profiles.

The nutrient profiles must be based on scientific knowledge about diet and nutrition, and their relation to health.

Before making regulations to establish nutrient profiles, the appropriate authority must request scientific advice from and expert committees and the authority must also carry out consultations with relevant authorities and interested parties in particular food business operators and consumer groups.

The appropriate authority is in England, the Secretary of State, in Wales, the Welsh Ministers and in Scotland, the Scottish Ministers. The Secretary of State can make regulations for GB with the consent of the Welsh and Scottish Ministers.

General conditions of use

Article 5 prescribes the general conditions of use for nutrition and health claims.

These include the beneficial nutritional or physiological effect of the food or nutrient which must be based on "generally accepted scientific evidence".

There are other general conditions of use specified in Article 5 including that the nutrient or substance for which the claim is made must be contained in the final product in a significant quantity and in a form that is available to be used by the body. The specific conditions of use applicable to nutrition and health claims must also be complied with.

The use of nutrition and health claims is only be permitted if the average consumer can be expected to understand the beneficial effects as expressed in the claim.

Nutrition and health claims must refer to the food ready for consumption in accordance with the manufacturer's instructions.

The FBO must be able to justify any claims they use and the competent authority may request the FBO or other person placing a product on the market to produce all relevant information establishing compliance with Regulation 1924/2006 (see Article 6).

Nutrition claims – specific requirements

Nutrition claims – introduction

A nutrition claim may only be made if it is contained in the Annex and its conditions of use are complied with (Article 8).

Nutrition claims set out in the Annex include: low energy, low fat; low sodium/salt; high fibre; high protein; high (followed by a reference to a specified vitamin or mineral).

The Annex states that the permitted nutrition claim (e.g. source of fibre) "and any claim likely to have the same meaning for the consumer" must comply with the specified conditions of use. Therefore, to say "contains fibre" might have the same meaning as "source of fibre" and can only be used if the conditions of use for "source of fibre" are fulfilled.

Comparative claims (Article 9)

The amended Article 9 in the retained NHCR states:

1. Without prejudice to the Business Protection from Misleading Marketing Regulations 2008, a comparison may only be made between foods of the same category, taking into consideration a range of foods of that category. The difference in the quantity of a nutrient and/or the energy value shall be stated and the comparison shall relate to the same quantity of food.

2. Comparative nutrition claims shall compare the composition of the food in question with a range of foods of the same category, which do not have a composition which allows them to bear a claim, including foods of other brands.

Health claims

Health claims – introduction

Article 10 (1) of the retained EU law states:

> "Health claims shall be prohibited unless they comply with the general requirements in Chapter II and the specific requirements in this Chapter and are authorised in accordance with this Regulation and are included in the list of authorised claims in the Annex to Commission Regulation (EU) 432/2012 or are authorised for the purposes of Article 14.

Reference may also be made to the GB Nutrition and Health Claims register referred to above.

Certain specified information must be included in the labelling, or where there is no labelling, in the presentation and advertising (Article 10 (2)):

(a) a statement indicating the importance of a varied and balanced diet and a healthy lifestyle;

(b) the quantity of the food and pattern of consumption required to obtain the claimed beneficial effect;

(c) where appropriate, a statement addressed to persons who should avoid using the food; and

(d) an appropriate warning for products that are likely to present a health risk if consumed to excess.

Examples of authorised health claims are; calcium is needed for the maintenance of normal bones, vitamin C contributes to the reduction of tiredness and fatigue and zinc contributes to the maintenance of normal bones.

A health claim relates to the nutrient, substance, food or food category for which they have been authorised and must not be made for the food product that contains them.

For example, it is proposed to use the health claim "thiamine contributes to the normal function of the heart" on a food supplement. Care must be taken to ensure that the claim as made on the label clearly is based on the presence of thiamine and does not relate to the product as a whole. This may be done by listing the authorised health claim immediately followed by the name of the ingredient to which it relates or perhaps by listing the authorised health claim immediately followed by an asterix or another symbol which is then placed next to the ingredient subject to the claim listed elsewhere on the label.

In addition, the conditions of use relating to the quantity of thiamine in the product must also be fulfilled.

It is possible to move away from the actual wording of the authorised health claim, some examples of which are quite scientific and technical, in the interests of better consumer understanding.

However, any changes to the wording must have the same meaning for the consumer as the authorised claim and care must be taken not to enhance or embellish the authorised wording.

Using the above example, "thiamine contributes to the normal function of the heart". Changing the wording to "thiamine makes your heart stronger" or "thiamine will improve the condition of your heart" may be seen as moving too far away from the meaning of the authorised claims and may, depending on context, be seen as making a medicinal claim by reference to curing, healing or preventing heart disease.

As with many labelling and food information issues, the words used and the context in which they are used, will be important in assessing compliance.

Finally, Article 10 (3) states that reference to general, non-specific benefits of the nutrient or food for overall good health or health-related well-being may only be made if accompanied by an authorised specific health claim.

Guidelines in respect of the application of specific conditions for health claims in Article 10 are contained in Commission Implementing Decision 2013/63/EU. This is particularly useful in respect of Article 10 (3) general claims in respect of which the Decision states that the specific authorised claim must bear some relevance to the general claim (therefore the broader the general claim, the easier it might be to create a link between it and the specific authorised claim). The Decision also states that the reference to the general claim must be accompanied by the specific claim. The concept of "accompanied" was considered in *Dr Willmar Schwabe GmbH & Co. KG v Queisser Pharma GmbH & Co. KG Case C-524/18.*

Restrictions on the use of certain heath claims – Article 12

Certain health claims are prohibited:

(a) claims which suggest that health could be affected by not consuming the food;

(b) claims which make reference to the rate or amount of weight loss;

(c) claims which make reference to recommendations of individual doctors or health professionals and associations other than national associations of medical, nutrition or dietetic professionals and health-related charities.

The prohibition in (c) can be problematic and requires careful consideration about the person involved and whether the claim refers to them making a recommendation. Guidance can be found on the Gov.UK nutrition law website.

Types of health claims

The main types of health claims are:

1. Function health claims (Article 13 (1))

- Relating to the growth, development and functions of the body

  (e.g. calcium is needed for the maintenance of normal teeth;

- Referring to psychological and behavioural functions

  (e.g. magnesium contributes to normal psychological function); and

- Slimming or weight-control

(e.g. substituting one daily meal of an energy restricted diet with a meal replacement contributes to the maintenance of weight after weight loss)

2. *Function health claims based on newly developed scientific evidence (Article 13 (5))*

3. *Risk reduction claims (Article 14 (1) (a)*

   - Reducing a risk factor in the development of a disease (e.g., reduction of blood cholesterol which is a risk factor in the development of coronary heart disease")

4. *Claims relating to children's development (Article 14 (1) (b)*

   - For example, vitamin D is needed for the normal growth and development of bone in children

5. *Claims about general or non-specific benefits (Article 10 (3))*

   - For example. "good for you" or "healthy" (see above)

The following case is an example of an application for a health claim which although it met the application criteria was not authorised.

In *Dextro Energy GmbH & Co KG v European Commission* (*T-100/15),* EFSA had confirmed that claims, relating to glucose, had met the necessary scientific criteria but the Commission had refused to authorise them. The Court of Justice of the European Union ruled in support of the Commission by saying it had not erred in principle in refusing to authorise the claims given that they were incompatible with generally accepted principles of nutrition and health which include a reduction in sugar consumption.

Conclusion

The general principle requiring claims to be authorised for consumer protection continues to apply in GB.

The mechanics of the authorisation process has changed but only time will tell whether GB's application of the risk criteria will be significantly different to the EU procedures.

There is no doubt that the GB model provides scope for the grant of authorisations that might not happen in the EU and there is the facility to move ahead on nutrient profiles.

As with most legal and regulatory issues, the question of divergence will arise.

Great Britain may choose to create its own regulatory criteria but in doing so it must have regard to, but not necessarily be bound by, what is happening in the EU and further afield. This may allow GB to be different but not that different.

CHAPTER SEVEN

TRACEABILITY, WITHDRAWAL AND RECALLS

Introduction

A food business operator (FBO) may become involved, at any time and without warning, in a problem concerning a food or ingredient they have received, made or supplied. This can make it a "crisis" for the business, or businesses involved.

Although the word crisis is often used in these situations, I have chosen use the word incident in this chapter.

The FBO may be required to act immediately, and may be expected to do so, whether or not they are in any way at fault, if they can intervene to help protect consumers.

The way in which the FBO responds to an incident will have a direct effect (either positive or negative) on them and their business. The manner and effectiveness of the response will, to a large extent, be determined by the way in which the FBO is ready to meet the challenges of a food incident.

This chapter will consider the measures that FBOs should have in place to enable them to respond swiftly and to effectively the meet the challenges of the situation.

The retained EU legislation

The rules relating to traceability, withdrawal and recall are contained in Articles 18 and 19 of regulation 178/2002 which has already been referred to in chapter 3 in the context of food safety.

There have only been a couple of minor amendments to Article 18 and 19 as a result of the UK's departure from the EU.

Types of food incidents

The following examples show the wide variety of issues and products that can be involved in a food incident.

Bacteria

Salmonella (chocolate), listeria (cheese), clostridium botulinum (pâté), campylobacter (chicken salad)

Physical

Plastic (ice cream), unauthorised gelling agent – choking hazard (jelly cups), rubber (curry), glass (pasties), moths/larvae (porridge flakes)

Labelling – allergens

Undeclared sesame (bread), undeclared prawns – crustaceans (salmon product), undeclared milk (chicken), undeclared mustard (spaghetti)

Labelling – other

Incorrect use-by date

Production

Food produced in unhygienic conditions (sandwiches) or in unapproved premises (meat)

Information about incidents is published on competent authorities' websites and elsewhere, and may be categorised as a food incident or an allergy incident,

Food business operators, particularly those working for larger organisations, are also likely to be aware of food incidents relevant to their organisations via internal sources.

Legal obligations

General

The key issues for FBOs are:

- The ability to identify the source of and destination of ingredients and products (traceability);
- Preventing affected foods from reaching consumers (withdrawal);
- Where affected products may have reached consumers telling them about the problem and prevent consumption (consumer information);
- Where other measures will not achieve a high level of public health protection recover affected product from consumers (recall);
- Working with other FBOs and the competent authorities to provide information about the affected product (cooperation and collaboration)

Traceability – Article 18

Article 18 (1) states: "The traceability of food, feed, food-producing animals, and any other substance intended to be, or expected to be, incorporated into a food or feed shall be established at all stages of production, processing and distribution."

Article 18 (4) states: "Food or feed which is placed on the market or is likely to be placed on the market in Great Britain shall be adequately labelled or identified to facilitate its traceability, through relevant documentation or information in accordance with the relevant requirements of more specific provisions."

The obligation in Article 18 is for the FBO to be able to identify from whom food or ingredients have been obtained and to whom food and ingredients have been supplied, and to put in place systems and procedures to allow that information to be provided to the competent authorities.

This is often referred to as the ability to trace products "one-step forward" and "one-step back".

FBOs are not required to have procedures to identify customers when they are the final consumer, although they may need to communicate directly with consumers via retailers or other methods.

Article 18 is worded in terms of its goal and intended result, rather than prescribing how that is to be achieved. In practice, the FBO will adopt a system which records the supplier from whom it obtained the product and the immediate customer along the food to chain to whom it supplies products.

FBOs will use approved suppliers that they have checked, and possibly physically audited, to ensure that the supplier is operating proper procedures.

Problems may arise when FBOs obtain products outside of its approved supplier network. They lose control over the products that enter the food premises and this can introduce uncontrolled hazards such as an unplanned and unexpected allergen which can be the source of a food incident.

Where FBOs are involved in food manufacture they bring many ingredients into an establishment and combine them to make intermediate or final products which are then supplied to other FBOs or to final consumers.

FBOs should ensure that they are able to trace how these ingredients are used within their food production operations. This will enable them to quickly identify a suspect ingredient or food, or a particular batch of suspect food. In the event of a food incident, the FBO may be able to limit the damage if the problem can easily be traced to a particular ingredient or process. This in turn will save time, money and resources, and protect consumers.

If this cannot be done quickly and easily the FBO may need to quarantine and/or destroy a much larger quantity of food. An inability to identify the affected ingredient or product may result in the FBO never quite knowing with any degree of certainty when all the suspect product or ingredient has been quarantined and removed from the market. One key aspect of resolving an incident is knowing when it is over and this becomes harder when the exact quantity of affected product is unknown.

The difference between identifying and dealing with one affected batch and with an unknown quantity of suspect food can be hugely significant in terms of FBO resources, loss of customer trust and the reaction of the competent authorities. The inability to be certain about the quantity of affected food may increase the likelihood of legal proceedings (civil and criminal) and the absence of proper documentation will greatly reduce the chances of robustly defending those proceedings.

On the flip side, a good, workable robust traceability system (external and internal) will give the FBO confidence to know that it is doing all it can to minimise the risks of problems arising and that it can react swiftly and effectively in the event that it becomes involved in a food incident, whether or not of its own making.

Traceability information

The type of information to meet Article 18 obligations includes:

- Name and address of supplier/customer and identification of the product;
- Date and time of the delivery/other transaction;
- Quantity of product; and
- A reference number or batch code for product in and out

This information must be made available to the competent authority on demand.

Food of animal origin is subject to specific traceability requirements as set out in Commission Implementing Regulation No 931/2011 (applicable in GB as retained EU law). The following information must be obtained and upon request provided to the competent authority "without undue delay":

- An accurate description of the food;
- The volume or quantity of the food;
- The name and address of the food business operator from which the food has been dispatched;
- The name and address of the consignor (owner) if different from the food business operator from which the food has been dispatched;
- The name and address of the food business operator to whom the food is dispatched;
- The name and address of the consignee (owner), if different from the food business operator to whom the food is dispatched;
- A reference identifying the lot, batch or consignment, as appropriate; and
- The date of dispatch.

Food Business Operators' responsibilities – Article 19

The provisions of Article 19 remain unchanged as a result of the UK having left the EU and the guiding principles of taking appropriate action to protect consumers remain applicable in GB.

The starting point for assessing the need to take action is whether the FBO "considers or has reason to believe that a food which it has imported, produced, processed, manufactured or distributed is not in compliance with the food safety requirements".

The FBO's obligation under Article 19 to withdraw food arises when:

1. The food in question is considered unsafe by the operator as not being in compliance with the food safety requirements; and

2. The food is on the market and has left the immediate control of the initial food business.

The reference to food safety requirements includes "unsafe food" as defined in Article 14.

The concept of immediate control is important. If all the affected food is identified while still in the food premises (e.g. it has been spotted in the production area or warehouse) and can be quarantined on site, Article 19 obligations may not apply.

That does not mean the situation should be ignored; the FBO will undertake a thorough review of its processes and procedures and take such steps as are necessary to prevent recurrence.

Affected food will have left the immediate control of a food business operator when it has been sold or supplied to a wholesaler or it is with any other FBO further along the food distribution chain.

If a FBO considers or has reason to believe that its food is not in compliance with the food safety requirements, and therefore unsafe, and has left its immediate control, what must it do?

- It must immediately initiate procedures to withdraw the food in question and inform the competent authorities;

- If that food may have reached the consumer, the FBO must "effectively and accurately" inform consumers the reason for the withdrawal;

- If the food has been supplied to consumers, the FBO must take such measures to achieve a high level of health protection which may involve recalling those products;

- Where an FBO considers or has reason to believe that a food that it has placed on the market may be "injurious to human health", the FBO must immediately inform the competent authorities of the action taken to prevent risks to the final consumer;

- An FBO must cooperate in actions taken by others and must collaborate with the competent authorities on action to avoid or prevent, reduce or eliminate a risk from the food.

Although withdrawal is not defined in the legislation its purpose is to remove from the food supply chain products which are not actually in the possession of consumers by preventing the distribution, display or offer of an affected product.

Practical application – a typical food incident

As each situation is unique, there may be no such thing as a "typical" food incident, but the following points may be of general application.

Awareness of a problem

As a food incident is an unplanned and unexpected event, the FBO cannot predict when one will happen. Perhaps no more than apocryphally, a food incident will occur late on a Friday afternoon, near or during holiday periods, when the business is on wind down at the end of a busy week. It may also occur when key members of the incident management team are away from the business.

The FBO must therefore be ready to respond swiftly and effectively at any time.

<u>The FBO's first response</u>

Don't panic! Now is the time for considered, clear and careful decision-making.

The incident management plan (also referred to as the crisis management plan) will have identified the most likely methods of communication with the business in times of an incident. This may be by e-mail, social media, and telephone, or following a visit by officials from the competent authority.

The first person within the business who is likely to be the first to hear about an incident must be trained to respond appropriately and immediately. This person may be the receptionist, anyone having access to the public e-mail address or anyone monitoring the organisation's social media outlets. The problem may be raised by a staff member who has seen something untoward during production.

The challenges and restrictions resulting from the Covid-19 pandemic means that many people continue to work remotely. Procedures should be reviewed to ensure that the same level of response can be given by and to key members of staff who are working remotely as would be the case if the they were physically working on site.

Unless the first communication is from the competent authorities, the initial message may not include words such as, "unsafe", "food safety requirement", "withdrawal", "recall", "injurious to health", "unfit for human consumption" or "Article 19 of the General Food Law Regulation"! If the complaint is from a trade customer, then the nature of the problem may be clearer.

In the case of an initial communication coming from a consumer the FBO must have trained its staff to identify words or phrases that might require an immediate response in line with the incident management plan.

How this is done depends on the nature and size of the business. Should all potential food incidents be directed immediately to a particular manager or director, at least in the first instance so they are aware of the issue? In one sense it does not matter to whom the matter is directed as long as they are fully aware of what they need to do next.

Whilst the actual mechanics of the response are business-specific it is essential that some positive action is taken. It would be unacceptable and potentially very damaging for the business, and for consumers, if there is a delay between receipt of the notification and the FBO's first response.

If there is any doubt as to the seriousness of the situation following initial notification, the business may wish to initiate the incident management procedure. It can always be halted very quickly and the worst-case scenario is staff are left a little red faced if indeed there was no incident. This is preferable to failing to act and allowing the situation to get out of control.

The FBO's next response

Assuming that the issue has been immediately passed to the relevant in-house person, they need to assess how to respond.

This will involve establishing the full facts. Although this may take a little time it is essential that the correct facts are properly obtained and understood otherwise valuable time, and resources, can be wasted in pursuing a line of enquiry that is not in fact related to the issue of concern.

What information is required?

As much information about the product and the allegation should be obtained.

The initial discussions with the complainant, with the competent authority or with the FBO's own staff will, hopefully, have identified the product and, due to clear labelling and documentation, the lot or batch number of which it is a part. This will enable to FBO to interrogate its own records to identify the extent of the problem; when was the product made, which production line was used and can the problem be limited to a single batch or has a significant amount of affected food left the premises.

Next steps

The FBO may need to physically examine the production equipment and/or the maintenance records. It may be necessary to review the production process and check various documents including cooking, cooling, reheating, storage, handling records to see if any of these processes are outside the specifications prescribed in the food safety management system for example, was a product stored at the wrong temperature leading to the growth of harmful pathogens or has a piece of machinery been damaged leading to plastic or metal potentially contaminating the food?

Communication

Once the extent of the problem has been properly established the FBO must decide who needs to be aware of the issue and how this is to be done.

This may include; people within the food business and related organisations, the supplier of an affected ingredient, the competent authority and/or downstream customers, retailers and consumers.

How the FBO handles communication to and from relevant stakeholders, including the media, will be highly significant in minimising the impact of the problem for the business and for consumers.

In respect of each communication, the clarity of the message is vital. There is a problem, or a suspected problem, and the FBO must explain what has happened, which product is affected, what is the problem (the hazard and the risk to consumers) and what should people who have purchased the problem do next (i.e. not consume it, return to place of purchase of a full refund etc.).

Any communication with the competent authority should be done as soon as reasonably possible when the FBO is able to provide full information about the extent of the problem and what action it is taking to protect consumers.

In a serious case, it may be necessary to provide initial details to the competent authority while explaining what action the FBO is taking to effectively resolve the situation. Ideally the FBO wants to be the first person to inform the competent authority, or if the authority already knows, the FBO wants to provide reassurance as soon as possible that it has the situation under control.

Even if the FBO is not satisfied that it is required to act under Article 19, there may be merit in telling the competent authority about the problem and outlining what action the FBO is taking. This could be done by way of an informal telephone call. It is far better for the business to be the first to tell the authority rather than them hearing it from another source.

If the product may have reached consumers the FBO must decide how to inform them of the problem. This may be by way of a recall notice at the point of sale, on a page on the FBO's website, via social media or, in a particularly serious or urgent case by radio or television.

Where the FBO is the manufacturer or producer of the affected product which has been supplied to retailers, it is essential that the retailer is told very clearly what to do and the first FBO needs to be satisfied that the retailer has done what is required to remove the product from the shelves. This will mean doing more than sending an e-mail in the hope that the retailer has read it and has taken the required steps. Following up the e-mail sent to the retailer with a telephone call or personal visit will provide assurance that matters are being dealt with properly.

As the investigation progresses the withdrawal or recall may expand to include other batches of the same product or even new products.

Finalising the incident

It is important that the FBO knows how much affected product has been supplied to retailers, how much has been sold and how much is to be taken off the shelves and returned to the FBO. Inconsistencies or inaccuracies at this stage could lead to affected product remaining on the market with the potential of being consumed.

Once the FBO has dealt with the initial flurry of activity they will have to do a number of things including: undertaking a thorough review and take action to prevent recurrence and/or identify other weaknesses in its systems (possibly reviewing and revising the HACCP system); repairing any reputational damage and restoring consumer confidence; compensating consumers or responding to claims for damages and/or being ready to respond to a formal investigation by the competent authorities and being prepared for increased scrutiny from the competent authorities, suppliers and customers.

A withdrawal or recall is never over until it is over and this only happens when the FBO is satisfied that it has taken all steps to remove affected product from the market and/or take such steps as are necessary to protect consumers.

Incident management teams and plans

Food business operators should establish incident management plans and incident management teams.

The plan will set out the steps to be taken in the event of a food incident. Staff should be trained to respond in accordance with the plan.

The incident management team will be determined by the size of the organisation and the extent of its activities but is should include a senior officer who can make decisions including signing off on communications, notifying the competent authority and authorising expenditure. Other members of the team might include the quality director, sales director, heads of the relevant departments, PR adviser (they may be internal or external), food lawyer or food regulatory adviser and someone to make notes and keep a timeline of when key decisions were taken and by whom.

In a cross-border situation, the FBO will need equivalent resources from its representatives or agents in local markets where the affected product has been distributed.

The team will need suitable facilities in which to work, including computers and access to refreshments; responding to an incident may require late night working!

Incident management plans should be tested and information about incident management teams should be kept updated (particularly to check that the personnel listed as being part of the team still work with the organisation!).

Conclusion

The basic obligations to be able to trace food, notify the competent authorities and warn consumers has remained largely unchanged since IP completion day.

It is essential that FBOs and their advisers ensure that they are ready to meet any challenges created by being involved in a food incident. They need to act quickly and decisively. Their incident management preparations will hopefully support the business and its staff and get the incident under control before damage can be caused to the business and, more importantly, consumers are not put at risk.

Regular testing of the incident management plan with the incident management team will help to iron out any issues and will give the business confidence to respond effectively if a major incident does arise. This does not have to a full-blown test; a desktop exercise can be beneficial.

If the FBO does not act when it should, the competent authority will step in and take steps to protect consumers. This will not be a good outcome for the business and failure to act properly is likely to increase the chances of regulatory or enforcement action being taken.

Finally, the FBO must examine its insurance policy to identify what is and what is not covered in the event of them becoming involved in a food incident requiring withdrawal and/or recall of product and the instruction of appropriate legal and regulatory advisers.

CHAPTER EIGHT

OFFICIAL CONTROLS AND ENFORCEMENT

Introduction

Rules designed to protect consumers must be clear and they must be easy to understand and apply by all stakeholders.

Those rules must be enforced rigorously but fairly, proportionately, based on risk, transparently and, perhaps above all, consistently.

The departure of the UK from the EU has created difficulties for businesses and consumers. It has also created significant challenges for the competent authorities and a collaborative approach to compliance, regulation and enforcement in the months ahead.

This chapter will consider how food law is enforced, short of prosecution, and the following chapters will look at food law as part of the criminal justice system and the regime for sentencing offenders.

Despite all the changes since IP completion day (11 pm 31 December 2020), the regime for domestic enforcement procedures has remained largely unaffected.

Businesses are still required to register or be approved, environmental health officers, trading standards officers and other authorised officers are still carrying out official controls, responding to complaints and serving notices.

It is business as usual in that regard.

Official Controls – Regulation 2017/625

In addition to powers contained in domestic regulations regard should be had to the provisions of Regulation 2017/625 on official controls (retained EU law).

The Regulation is detailed and includes customs provisions about entry of animals and goods into Great Britain, border controls posts and related matters (which are outside the scope of this book).

The Regulation lays down rules relating to, amongst other things:

- The performance of official controls and other official activities by the competent authorities of Great Britain; and
- The adoption of conditions to be fulfilled with respect to animals and goods entering Great Britain from a third country.

    (Article 1 (1))

A third country is defined as "any country or territory outside the British Islands" (Article 3 (2D)).

The term "British Islands" is defined in the Interpretation Act 1978 as "the United Kingdom, the Channel Island and the Isle of Man"

The Regulation applies to the official controls performed for the verification of compliance with the rules in the areas specified in Article 1 (2) including:

- Food and food safety, integrity and wholesomeness;
- Feed and feed safety;
- Fair practices in trade and protecting consumer interests and information;
- Animal health and welfare;

- Organic production and labelling
- The use and labelling of protected designations of origin, protected geographical indications and traditional specialities guaranteed.

Article 2 states that official controls are activities performed by the competent authorities, or by the delegated bodies or the natural persons to which certain official control tasks have been delegated in accordance with this Regulation, in order to verify:

(a) compliance by the operators with this Regulation and with the rules referred to in Article 1(2); and

(b) that animals or goods meet the requirements laid down in the rules referred to in Article 1(2), including for the issuance of an official certificate or official attestation.

The competent authorities are those designated as such in the particular subject-matter legislation such as a local authority, the FSA or FSS.

As observed elsewhere in this book, the "appropriate authority" is; in England, the Secretary of State, in Wales, the Welsh Ministers and in Scotland, the Scottish Ministers.

When non-compliance is suspected, competent authorities are required to perform an investigation in order to confirm or to eliminate that suspicion (Article 137).

Where non-compliance is established, the competent authorities shall take:

(a) any action necessary to determine the origin and extent of the non-compliance and to establish the operator's responsibilities; and

(b) appropriate measures to ensure that the operator concerned remedies the non-compliance and prevents further occurrences of such non-compliance.

When deciding which measures to take, the competent authorities shall take account of the nature of that non-compliance and the operator's past record with regard to compliance (Article 138 (1)).

The measures available to the competent authority are set out in Article 138 (2) and include the following:

- order treatments on goods, the alteration of labels or corrective information to be provided to consumers;
- restrict or prohibit the placing on the market, the movement, the entry into Great Britain or the export of animals and goods; and prohibit, or order their return to, the country of dispatch;
- require the operator to increase their own controls or to increase the official controls;
- order the recall, withdrawal, removal and destruction of goods, authorising, where appropriate, the use of the goods for purposes other than those for which they were originally intended;
- order the closure of a business, suspend its activities or suspend or withdraw registration or approval

Article 139 states that penalties shall be "effective, proportionate and dissuasive" and that financial penalties for violations of this Regulation and of the rules referred to in Article 1(2), perpetrated through fraudulent or deceptive practices, reflect, in accordance with national law, at least either the economic advantage for the operator or, as appropriate, a percentage of the operator's turnover.

Regulation 2017/625, was amended by Official Controls (Animals, Feed and Food, Plant Health etc.) (Amendment) (EU Exit) Regulations 2020/1481.

Principles of enforcement

Resources relevant to enforcement include the Food Standards Agency's Food Law Code of Practice and Food Law Practice Guidance documents.

The ones for England were issued in March 2021 and reference Regulation 2017/625 on official controls mentioned above. Similar documents are available for Wales, Scotland and Northern Ireland.

Competent authorities must:

- ensure that enforcement action taken by their authorised officers is:
  - in accordance with Chapter 6 of the Practice Guidance
  - reasonable
  - proportionate
  - risk-based
  - consistent with good practice
- take account of the following when considering whether to initiate enforcement action:
  - the Code for Crown Prosecutors
  - the Competent Authority's enforcement policy
  - the Regulators' Code
  - the nature of the non-compliance and the FBO's past record regarding compliance
  - whether a Primary Authority Partnership is in place, and of any Primary Authority Advice issued
- ensure the reasons for any departure from the criteria set out in the Competent Authority's enforcement policy are documented

(section 6.2 of the FSA Food Law Code):

Unless the competent authority, or more often the relevant officer on the ground, determines that the breach has created a serious and immediate risk, the authority will often approach the matter by reference to the hierarchy of enforcement.

This requires the authority to take account of the full range of enforcement options available such as education, giving advice, informal action, formal action (serving notices), and prosecution.

When responding to a competent authority, it may be possible to argue that the action, or proposed action, is unnecessary and disproportionate, or is not supported by sufficient evidence.

However, enforcement action will prioritise interventions that are necessary to prevent or minimise risks to humans, animals, plants and the environment.

Authorised officers

Enforcement action, such as issuing enforcement notices, may only be done by an officer who had been duly authorised by the particular competent authority. Checking that the officer has been properly authorised and was authorised at the appropriate time to enforce the particular legislation is an essential first step.

It is also important to check the regulations to see if they specify which organisation is the competent authority for the particular action taken by the officer. This might sound obvious, but some regulations provide that the competent authority for one function is organisation X and for another function the competent authority is organisation Y. X cannot undertake actions in respect of functions in respect of which it is not the competent authority and X's officers cannot act in respect of matters where X is not the competent authority.

In this regard, reference may be made to the Welfare of Animals at the Time of Killing (England) Regulations 2015, as amended.

It can often useful to try and establish the officer's level of experience as the issuing of enforcement notices often depends on the relevant officer's opinion based on their assessment of facts they have observed.

The definition of "authorised officer" can be found in the particular legislation and by way of example, Regulation 2 of the Food Safety and Hygiene (England) Regulations 2013 states:

> *""authorised officer", in relation to an enforcement authority, means any person (whether or not an officer of the authority) who is authorised by them in writing, either generally or specially, to act in matters arising under the Hygiene Regulations and Regulation 178/2002;"*

Powers of authorised officers

Once the officer has been properly authorised, they may only act in accordance with powers contained in the legislation under consideration. It is therefore necessary to carefully review that legislation to check that any official action is within the scope of those powers.

For example, Regulation 16 (1) of the 2013 Regulations states:

> *"An authorised officer of a food authority, on producing, if so required, some duly authenticated document showing authorisation, has a right at all reasonable hours*

(a) *to enter any premises within the authority's area for the purpose of ascertaining whether there is or has been on the premises any contravention of the provisions of the Hygiene Regulations or Regulation 178/2002;*

(b) *to enter any premises, whether within or outside the authority's area, for the purpose of ascertaining whether there is on the premises any evidence of any such contravention within that area; and*

(c) *to enter any premises for the purpose of the performance by the authority of their functions under the Hygiene Regulations or Regulation 178/2002,*

> *but admission to any premises used only as a private dwelling-house may not be demanded as of right unless 24 hours' notice of the intended entry has been given to the occupier."*

The same powers are given to an authorised officer of the Food Standards Agency (see Regulation 16 (2)).

Most officials will introduce themselves by reference to their name, occupation (e.g. as an EHO with Z Council) and produce some written evidence of their authority. The FBO should not be afraid of asking to see the "duly authenticated document" and the officer should be able to provide this without difficulty. The FBO should make a note of the officer's name.

Entry to premises may also be made under the powers of a court warrant which may be granted if a justice of the peace, on sworn information in writing, is satisfied that the criteria in Regulation 16 (3) are met namely:

1) There is a reasonable ground for entry for purposes set out in Regulation 16 (1) or 16 (2) and either;

2) Admission to the premises has been refused, or a refusal is apprehended, and that notice of the intention to apply for a warrant has been given to the occupier; or

3) An application for admission, or the giving of such notice, would defeat the object of the entry, or the case is one of urgency, or that the premises are unoccupied, or the occupier is temporarily absent.

Reasonable force may be used to gain entry under the power of a warrant.

The FBO, or their representative should retain a copy of the warrant and note any explanation for the entry given by the officers. Making immediate contact with their food law adviser is crucial and in due course the circumstances around the application for and grant of the warrant may be investigated and challenged.

The officer may be accompanied by "such other persons as the officer considers necessary". This may include a police constable or someone with expertise in the subject-matter of the investigation.

Once on the premises the officer may do whatever the applicable legislation prescribes. This may include:

1) Inspect records relating to the food business;

2) Obtain access to a computer where those records are held and to do so may require the assistance of a person in charge of, or using, the computer;

3) Seize and detain records which the officer has reason to believe may be required as evidence in proceedings under the provisions of the 2013 Regulations; and

4) In respect of records held electronically, require the records to be produced in a form in which they can be taken away

FBOs require a general awareness of what authorised officers can and cannot do because preventing the officer from carrying out their duties may amount to obstruction (a criminal offence).

FBOs should also keep notes of who comes onto their premises, what they see and who they speak with.

Enforcement notices

Food legislation provides a wide variety of enforcement notices that may be issued by authorised officers on behalf of competent authorities.

The form and content of the notice should be checked carefully for compliance with the applicable provisions of the relevant legislation.

In addition, reference should be had to other documents such as the Food Standards Agency's Food Law Code and Guidance which provide examples of the different types of notices and the circumstances in which they should, and should not, be used.

Enforcement notices available to competent authorities include:

1) Improvement Notice (section 10 Food Safety Act 1990 – a very important provision in the context of appeals in respect of various food regulations e.g. food information)

2) Hygiene Improvement Notice (Regulation 6 of the 2013 Regulations);

3) Hygiene Emergency Prohibition Notice (Regulation 8 of the 2013 Regulations);

4) Remedial Action Notice (Regulation 9 of the 2013 Regulations); and

5) Detention Notice (Regulation 10 of the 2013 Regulations).

Non-compliance with a large number of enforcement notices is a criminal offence.

The officer issuing the notice must have formed a view about the degree of non-compliance by reference to the provisions of the legislation, and in due course will be require to substantiate that view, for example:

1) If an authorised officer has *reasonable grounds* for believing that the proprietor of a food business is failing to comply with specified regulations (Improvement Notice – IN – section 10 FSA 1990);

2) If an authorised officer *is satisfied* that the health risk condition is fulfilled with respect to any food business (Hygiene Emergency Prohibition Notice – HEPN – regulation 8 of the 2013 Regulations); and

3) Where *it appears* to an authorised officer that in respect of premises requiring approval any of the requirements of the Hygiene Regulations is being breached or inspection under the Hygiene Regulations is being hampered (Remedial Action Notice – RAN – regulation 9 of the 2013 Regulations)

In all of these situations the officer must have gathered evidence that justified the appropriate state of mind necessary to issue the notice. If the FBO can show that the officer is wrong about the facts and/or misunderstood them and/or incorrectly applied them in the context of the legislation, there may be grounds for challenging the notice.

Responding to enforcement notices

As failure to comply with an enforcement notice is usually a criminal offence; doing nothing is not usually an option.

In addition to those criminal consequences, receiving an enforcement notice can have very serious consequences for the business. The effect of the notice might be to close the premises until the business has taken some specified action (e.g. with a HEPN the FBO must take action to remove the imminent risk of injury) or the activities may be curtailed (a RAN may prohibit the use of equipment or the carrying out of any process) and there may be some reputational damage.

How the FBO responds will depend on the circumstances existing at the time. The best course of action may be to undertake works as quickly as possible and to get the officer to certify that the necessary steps have been taken so the FBO can get back to "business as usual".

The FBO may take some immediate action in response to the notice but may feel sufficiently aggrieved to take matters further. This may be done in accordance with the competent authority's provisions for an internal appeal or it may be done by way of a formal appeal.

Appealing the notice

The notice should explain the mechanism for appealing the notice but the FBO and its advisers should nevertheless check the wording of the legislation, assuming there is a statutory power to appeal the notice, which is not always the case.

The appeal mechanism will be prescribed in the regulations and this usually involves appealing to the magistrates" court or the First-tier Tribunal.

The issues to consider include:

1. Is there a statutory power of appeal (if not is it possible to make a claim for judicial review and seek urgent injunctive relief) – see *The Queen on the application of Association of Independent Meat Suppliers v Food Standards Agency [2019] UKSC 36 and Case C-579/19*;

2. If there is a statutory power to appeal, the FBO must check certain things; what is the time limit for commencing the appeal, where is the appeal venue (usually the magistrates' court or the First-tier Tribunal – FTT) and what documents are required to commence the appeal;

3. Once the appeal is lodged the FBO needs to know how long before the appeal will be heard. Any delay in the appeal being heard by the court or FTT could have very serious consequences for the food business. If the appeal cannot be heard immediately or within a reasonable time, consideration should be given to seeking High Court relief to suspend the effect of the notice, at least in the short term.

Powers of the Magistrates' Court/First-tier Tribunal

<u>Magistrates' court</u>

The first hearing in the magistrates' court is likely to be used for giving directions for the substantive appeal hearing, the timing of which will depend on issues such as the urgency of the case, but more likely on court time and availability. Prior to sending the Complaint to the court it can often be prudent to liaise with the court office to establish the likely timeframe for a full hearing at that court or at another court centre.

Evidence of the inability of the court system to accommodate a full hearing within a reasonable period of time will be useful if seeking urgent relief in the High Court.

After hearing the parties and their evidence the magistrates' court "shall make the order for which the complaint is made or dismiss the complaint" (Section 53 (2) Magistrates' Courts Act 1980 – MCA).

First-tier Tribunal

The overriding objective of the FTT Procedure Rules is "to enable the Tribunal to deal with cases fairly and justly" (see rule 2 of the FTT Procedure Rules) and FTT has substantial case management powers to achieve this (see rule 5 of those Rules). The Tribunal will expect the parties to "help the Tribunal to further the overriding objective" and to "co-operate" with the Tribunal (Rule 2).

In an appropriate case, the FTT has the power to suspend the effect of the enforcement notice and such an application should be made within the body of the notice of appeal.

The FTT will send the notice of appeal and accompanying documents to the respondent competent authority and will in due course send the parties a list of directions which may include a suspension of the effect of the notice if this has been requested, and the FTT will ask the parties to provide dates of unavailability within a specified time period to assist in making arrangements for listing the appeal hearing.

Costs

The costs associated with an appeal against an enforcement notice are always a relevant factor for the FBO and for the competent authority.

One issue that needs to be canvassed with the client at the outset is whether, assuming they win, the "loser" will pay their costs.

In the magistrates' court, costs in civil cases, such as these types of appeals, are governed by the provisions of section 64 of the Magistrates'' Courts Act 1980. At the outcome of the appeal the court may make "such order as to costs" as "it thinks just and reasonable" by the "loser" to the "winner".

In the FTT, costs orders are not dependent on "losers" and "winners" as such. Rule 10 of the FTT Procedure Rules states that the Tribunal may make an order for costs only in respect of wasted costs or if the Tribunal considers that a party has acted unreasonably in bringing, defending or conducting the proceedings.

Further appeals

A person aggrieved by the dismissal of an appeal to the magistrates' court, remembering that it has determined the appeal acting in its civil jurisdiction, may appeal to the crown court (see for example, Section 38 Food Safety Act 1990 and Regulation 23 of the 2013 Regulations).

Appeals against a decision of the FTT to the Upper Tribunal are governed by Rule 39 of the FTT Procedure Rules which refer to appeals being brought on a point of law under section 11 of the Tribunals, Courts and Enforcement Act 2007. Permission to appeal to the Upper Tribunal must be sought by way of written application made to the FTT within 28 days of when the FTT sent the decision the subject of the application (Rule 42 of the FTT Procedure Rules).

It should be noted that it is possible to apply to have decisions of the FTT set aside or reviewed.

Conclusion

The key issues for the FBO and their legal advisers when considering how best to respond to enforcement action are: was the officer duly authorised to issue the notice; did they have the necessary belief, which must be based on evidence, are there sufficient legal grounds for issuing the notice, is the format and content of the notice compliant, is the notice clear in what is alleged to be the non-compliance and in what it requires the recipient to do and has it been served properly on the correct legal entity responsible for the alleged non-compliance (i.e. a company or an individual).

Deciding on the response to an enforcement notice is not always straightforward and requires careful consideration of all the relevant issues.

Whatever decision is taken it should only be reached after a careful assessment of all the options and implications and in doing so, the FBO should work in partnership with its food law advisers and appropriate experts.

CHAPTER NINE

CRIMINAL PROSECUTIONS

Introduction

Where food legislation creates criminal offences for non-compliance, those proceedings are subject to the general rules of criminal evidence and compliance with the Criminal Procedure Rules.

Non-compliance with the rules of evidence could result in the prosecution being unable to rely on crucial information it needs in order to prove its case.

Non-compliance with the Criminal Procedure Rules could have serious consequences for the prosecution and could result in an application for summonses being ruled to be a nullity and hence the court would lack jurisdiction to hear the case (see the discussion about this issue in *Food Standards Agency v Bakers of Nailsea Limited [2020] EWHC 3632 (Admin))*.

Food offences may be heard in the magistrates' court or in the crown court and the penalties can be very severe.

Prosecutions are usually taken by competent authorities against the food business operator (FBO) and where the FBO is a company, the law makes provision for proceedings to be taken against the company and, at the same time, against an individual such as a director, manager or similar person where they are responsible for the company's failure to comply with the law.

An individual may therefore be prosecuted because he or she is a director, or senior officer, of a corporate FBO or because he or she is an FBO in their own right.

Food law offences

Food legislation will specifically refer to those matters which create criminal offences and will also set out the maximum penalties (e.g. fines or imprisonment) that may be imposed

The vast majority of food law offences are classed as strict liability. The prosecution does not generally need to prove that the FBO intended to break the law, knew they were breaking the law or was reckless in the manner in which they conducted their activities which led to the contravention. Nevertheless, these issues will be relevant at any sentencing hearing (see the next chapter).

Reference must be made to the particular piece of legislation under consideration for the precise wording of the offence provisions and for the methods of punishing proven non-compliance.

The following are two examples based on legislation referred to elsewhere in this book.

Food Safety and Food Hygiene

Regulation 19(1) of the Food Safety and Hygiene (England) Regulations 2013 makes provision for criminal offences.

It states that any person who contravenes or fails to comply with any of the specified EU provisions, as defined, commits an offence.

In practice, the most common offences that come before the court include placing unsafe food on the market (Article 14 of Regulation 178/2002) and failing to comply with various hygiene rules contained in Regulations 852/2004 and 853/2004.

Food Information

The vast majority of breaches of Food Information Regulations 2014 (FIR) which give national effect to the EU Provision of Food Information to Consumers Regulation (Regulation 1169/2011), may only be enforced by means of an improvement notice.

Those breaches of the FIR that attract criminal liability are set out in Regulation 10 and relate to the failure to provide proper allergen information and these offences are summary only meaning that they may only be heard in the magistrates' court although the fine could still be quite significant.

Commencing a criminal prosecution

Criminal prosecutions should only be commenced after a thorough review of the case by the competent authority and its lawyers. They need to apply the criteria set out in the Code for Crown Prosecutors, the Full Code Test and decide that there is sufficient evidence to prosecute and that it is in the public interest to do so:

1) Is there enough evidence against the defendant or defendants in respect of each alleged offence?

   A criminal case depends on the prosecution adducing sufficient cogent, reliable, credible, admissible evidence to a court that is sufficient to provide a realistic prospect of conviction.

   There is either sufficient evidence or there is not. If there is insufficient evidence then the second question should not arise.

2) Is it in the public interest for the prosecution to bring the case to court?

   Once the prosecutor has determined that there is sufficient evidence then all the relevant factors must be weighed in the balance; some pointing towards a prosecution being commenced and some pointing the other way.

   Each case is different but some general matters to be taken into account are:

   <u>Factors pointing towards prosecution</u>

   A serious breach, actual harm or serious risk of harm to the public, significantly misleading consumers, the FBO having previous relevant convictions, the non-compliance having lasted for a long time, particularly in circumstances in which the FBO had been aware of the problem.

Factors pointing against prosecution

A minor breach, a first offence, a one-off set of unforeseeable circumstances not resulting in serious harm or risk of harm, taking swift and effective steps to remedy the problem, personal circumstances (illness, age).

Time limits

Criminal proceedings are usually commenced by the prosecutor making an application to the magistrates' court for the issue of a summons in accordance with the Criminal Procedure Rules (previously referred to as laying an information) or by way of a requisition.

The proceedings must be commenced "in time" (i.e. the application must be made within any statutory limitation period) and this should be checked by the competent authority and the court before issue and by the FBO and their advisers when summonses are served.

The basic principles applicable to time limits are that summary offences (triable only in the magistrates' court), must be brought within 6 months of the date when the offence was committed. Commencing cases that may be tried in the magistrates' court or the crown court is not usually subject to a time limit.

However, some food law offences that may be tried in the magistrates' court or the crown court are subject to specific time limits prescribed in the applicable legislation.

Time specified in the legislation

An example may be found in Regulation 18 of the Food Safety and Hygiene (England) Regulations 2013 which states:

"No prosecution for an offence under these Regulations which is punishable under paragraph (2) of regulation 19 shall be begun after the expiry of—

(a) three years from the commission of the offence; or

(b) one year from its discovery by the prosecutor,

whichever is the earlier."

<u>The impact of a Primary Authority relationship on time limits</u>

Where a food business has entered into a Primary Authority relationship with a local authority this has a, potentially significant, impact on the time period within which criminal proceedings must be commenced.

The relevant legal provisions are to be found in section 28 of the Regulatory Enforcement and Sanctions Act 2008 and related legislation.

The legislation states that an authority seeking to take enforcement action against a business must notify the Primary Authority of its intentions (save in urgent situations not relevant here).

The Primary Authority must consider the proposed enforcement action and review any advice it has given to the business before responding to the enforcing authority which it must do within 5 working days. If the proposed enforcement action can be taken the enforcing authority must inform the business which has 10 working days in which to respond and refer to matter to the Local Better Regulation Office.

During those 15 working days the enforcing authority may not take the proposed enforcement action, which includes prosecution. The practical effect of this is to extend the statutory period within which proceedings must be commenced by those 15 working days.

The investigation and the interview under caution

During the course of its investigation into an alleged breach of food law, the competent authority may invite the FBO or its representative to answer questions about the circumstances of the offence in an interview under caution conducted in accordance with the Police and Criminal Evidence act 1984 and related Codes of Practice.

This is an important part of the investigation as it allows the competent authority the opportunity to obtain evidence, or further evidence against the FBO.

It also allows the FBO to put its side of the story and present information to the authority that might persuade it not to prosecute the case.

The person to be interviewed should consult their legal adviser to plan the best approach which might be:

1. To attend the interview with their legal adviser and answer all the questions;

2. To attend the interview and submit a prepared statement written under caution and answer no questions;

3. To attend the interview and answer "no comment" to the questions or remain silent; or

4. To decline to attend the interview but submit a prepared statement under caution setting out the FBOs response to the allegation and providing details of their systems and procedures and explaining what went wrong and setting out the measures it has taken to prevent any recurrence.

There is no "right" response but it is becoming more common for FBOs to cooperate with the investigation by adopting the response at point 4 above and this procedure has been adopted by some regulators during the Covid-19 restrictions.

Challenges to the prosecution case – due diligence

The FBO may be able to challenge the factual basis for the prosecution case which may include showing gaps in the evidence or showing that the witnesses are wrong.

In addition, the FBO may be able to argue that they did everything that could reasonably have been expected for them to prevent the problem having occurred; the defence of due diligence.

Regulation 12 of the Food Safety and Hygiene (England) Regulations 2013 states that it is a defence for the FBO to prove that they, "took all reasonable precautions and exercised all due diligence to avoid the commission of the offence by the accused or by a person under the control of the accused."

Whether there is any merit in the FBO arguing this defence depends on all the facts and circumstances but, in discussion with their advisers, the following issues may need to be taken into account:

- The food business must have done something to prevent the offence occurring in the first place;
- All reasonable precautions requires the business to put in place a sufficient and robust food safety management system to prevent what allegedly happened from happening (see the earlier discussions around this and HACCP);
- All due diligence means that the business has put in place a sufficient and robust procedure for checking to ensure that the system is working correctly and to make appropriate changes if it is not;
- The systems and procedures should be written down and staff must be trained on them;
- Documents and records must be maintained;
- The systems and procedures must be capable of proactively preventing problems and reactively correcting them when required;
- Allocation of responsibilities in respect of the systems and procedures must be recorded;
- The systems and procedures must cover all aspects of the food business;
- The systems and procedures relied on for the due diligence defence must relate to the offence or offences before the court.

Where the FBO seeks to blame someone else for the offence they must provide the prosecutor with information "identifying or assisting in the identification" of that other person (Regulation 12 (5)).

The FBO will need to present evidence about its business and its systems and may require an expert to comment on them in light of what was in place and operating and, perhaps, to advise the court about the standards that are to be expected and the extent to which the FBO was complying with those standards.

The ideal expert is someone with perhaps four key qualities:

1. A sound knowledge and understanding of the topic;

2. The ability to write a thorough, well-researched report dealing with the issues;

3. The ability to explain that report and complex scientific evidence in a simple, straightforward and easy to understand manner; **and**

4. Someone who has the confidence to be able to identify when something is outside their area(s) expertise and who will not be tempted to discuss matters best left to others.

The final prerequisite for any expert is an understanding of the role and duties of the expert which are to "give opinion which is objective and unbiased" and which is "within the expert's area or areas of expertise".

Reference should always be had to Part 19 of the Criminal Procedure Rules 2020 which deals with expert evidence similar provisions relating to experts can be found in Part 35 of the Civil Procedure Rules).

Above all, the expert owes a duty to the court and not to the party that has instructed, and paid, them.

Conclusion

As most food law offences are strict liability there may be little opportunity to successfully defend them at trial. This does not mean that the FBO should not, where appropriate, challenge the prosecution case.

However, if the FBO has put in place well-documented and proper procedures and systems which have functioned correctly, it may be possible to show that there was not much else they could have done to comply with their obligations and the contravention occurred despite all these suitable measures being in place.

This may have three consequences; it may deter the competent authority from bringing a criminal prosecution, it may allow the FBO to argue the due diligence defence and it may be very relevant to any sentence that the court may impose.

CHAPTER TEN

SENTENCING

Introduction

The "Health and Safety Offences, Corporate Manslaughter and Food Safety and Hygiene Offences – Definitive Guideline" took effect on 1st February 2016 and the result has been a significant change in the way in which the parties and the courts approach sentencing in the majority of food law cases.

The Guideline was introduced in England and Wales because of a perception that sentences in food safety and hygiene cases were quite low coupled with inconsistencies in sentencing between different courts. This inconsistent approach made it hard to advise food businesses operators on the likely level of punishment.

The reality reflects a situation in which penalties for food law offences subject to the Guideline have increased since February 2016, particularly so for large organisations having a substantial turnover.

The Guideline may not have removed the perceived previous inconsistent sentencing, but it has allowed all parties, prosecution, the FBO and the court, to standardise, to a degree, the way in which sentencing hearings are prepared for and conducted.

This chapter will focus on the approach to sentencing required by the Guideline, although it does not apply to all food law offences.

Regard must also be had to the Sentencing Act 2020, which was in force from 1 December 2020 (the Sentencing Code).

The Guideline – general issues

Food law offences subject to the provisions of the Guideline include some of the matters referred to elsewhere in this book namely; placing unsafe food on the market, breaches of hygiene legislation, non-compliance with traceability requirements and breaches of the provisions regarding withdrawal and recall of unsafe foods.

Before looking at the Guideline in detail it should be noted that the law is slightly different between England and Wales.

In England the law on safety and hygiene has been combined in the Food Safety and Hygiene (England) Regulations 2013 whereas in Wales the law remains divided; the General Food Regulations 2004 and the Food Hygiene (Wales) Regulations 2006.

This has little impact when an organisation is being sentenced as it faces the possibility of an unlimited fine, albeit on which is subject to the application of the Guideline.

Under the 2013 England Regulations, an FBO who is an individual and is being sentenced by the magistrates' court may not be sent to prison; he or she may only be fined. In a particularly serious case, the inability of the magistrates' court to impose a custodial sentence may mean the case is sent to the crown court to be dealt with although this does not mean a prison sentence will be imposed.

In Wales an individual being sentenced in the magistrates' court for a food safety offence, and also for offences relating to traceability, withdrawal and recall, may be sent to prison for a term up to 6 months.

In both jurisdictions, the crown court may impose a maximum punishment of 2 years' imprisonment.

Although the Guideline provides a structured approach that the parties and the court must follow, it remains flexible enough to allow the court to have regard to all the relevant factors and impose a sentence that is appropriate in all the circumstances (for example see the comments at paragraph 12 in the case of *Whirlpool Appliances v Regina (HSE) [2017]* EWCA Crim 2186, as applied for example in *R (HSE) v ATE Truck and Trailer Sales Limited* [2018] EWCA Crim 752).

Sentencing of organisations

The Guideline clearly sets out how the structured approach is to apply but the following points are particularly relevant.

Step One – determining the offence category

The court must determine the offence category "using only the culpability and harm factors" that are set out on page 30 of the Guideline.

Culpability

There are 4 levels of culpability; very high, high, medium and low.

Category	Applicability
Very High	The most serious cases where there has been "a deliberate breach of or flagrant disregard for the law".
High	Offender fell far short of the appropriate standard (e.g. failing to put proper measures in place, allowing breaches to go on for a long time, serious/systematic failure to address risks to health and safety)
Medium	Offender fell short of the appropriate standard (e.g. systems were in place but not sufficiently adhered to or implemented)
Low	Offender did not fall far short of the appropriate standard (e.g. significant efforts to secure food safety, minor failings occurred as an isolated incident)

It is usually clear where a case is "very high" or "low" but the parties must carefully assess all the evidence to either agree whether the case is "high" or "medium" or to clearly set out their rival submissions for the benefit of the court.

Harm

Harm factors include actual harm and a risk of harm which involves a consideration of likelihood of harm and the extent of the harm if it does occur.

Death is not specifically mentioned as a harm factor. In its consultation document which preceded the definitive guideline, the Sentencing Council, stated that serious harm, including death, arising from food cases was a potential outcome this was, in practice, rare. Where death or very serious injury does occur, the court would be entitled to reflect this by moving outside the category range.

There are three categories of harm: 1, 2 and 3.

Category	Applicability
1	Serious adverse effects on individual(s) and/or having a widespread impact. High risk of an adverse effect on individual(s) including a supply to vulnerable groups.
2	Adverse effect on individual(s) not amounting to category 1. Medium risk of an adverse effect or low risk of a serious adverse effect. Regulator and/or legitimate industry substantially undermined.

	Relevant authorities unable to trace products or are otherwise inhibited in identifying or addressing risks to health. Consumer mislead regarding food's compliance with religious or personal beliefs.
3	Low risk of an adverse effect on individual(s). Public misled about the specific food consumed, but little or no risk of actual adverse effect on individuals.

Again, the parties may be able to agree the appropriate category but if not, the court will need clear submissions supported by evidence, possibly expert evidence, to assist it make a determination.

Even if the parties reach an agreement about culpability and harm, the court may still decide matters for itself.

Step 2 – Starting point and category range

The starting point fine is based on the organisation's annual turnover, or equivalent, and hence the provision of accounts to the court is crucial. Usually, the court will want to see three years' accounts in order to get a true picture of the organisation's financial situation.

If accounts are not produced or the court has doubt about the financial information that has been provided the court may infer that the organisation can pay any fine.

Although the court should only have regard to the financial situation of the organisation being sentenced, it may have regard to the resources of a "linked organisation" where they "can properly be taken into account" (see *Regina v Tata Steel UK Limited* [2017] EWCA Crim 704).

The Guideline contains four tables of fines based on the organisation's turnover:

- Large – turnover £50 million and over
- Medium – turnover between £10 million and £50 million
- Small – turnover between £2 million and £10 million
- Micro – turnover not more than £2 million

Organisations with a turnover that "greatly exceeds the threshold for large organisations" it may be necessary to move outside the suggested range to "achieve a proportionate sentence".

This does not mean that the court simply decides on a level of fine in the appropriate table and applies a multiplier based on the amount by which the turnover exceeds the £50 million figure for a "large" organisation (see *Whirlpool Limited* – above – at paragraph 34).

The Guideline does not differentiate between a "large" and a "very large" organisation, it simply says that with a very large organisation it might be necessary to move outside the range for large organisations.

As observed by the Court of Appeal in *R v Places for People Homes [2021] EWCA Crim 410,* the larger the company the greater the fine might need to be in order for it to be proportionate to the organisations' means, to constitute adequate punishment, and to bring home to management and shareholders the need for regulatory compliance. The extent to which any increase was required would depend upon the particular circumstances of each individual case and was not something for "mechanistic extrapolation" (paragraph 32 of the Judgment).

The Court in that case made reference to *R. v Thames Water Utilities Ltd [2015] EWCA Crim 960* and *R. v Thames Water Utilities Ltd [2019] EWCA Crim 1344.*

A fine imposed during a magistrates' court case in 2021 about unsafe food on display after its use by date raised more than a few eyebrows. In that case, Tesco Stores Limited was fined more than £7.5 million and ordered to pay prosecution costs of £95,500.00. The District Judge observed that that the Guideline does not adequately provide for very large organisations with a turnover exceeding £1 billion.

When representing a very large organisation, careful thought must be given to explaining to the judge, if necessary, why she or he should not significantly increase the level of fine *just because* the organisation has an exceptionally large turnover.

Within each of the four tables the Guideline provides a starting point fine and a range of fines.

By way of example:

In respect of a large organisation where the court's assessment of the case is high culpability with harm category 2, the starting point fine is £230,000.00 with a category range of between £90,000.00 and £600,000.00.

For a small organisation where the assessment of the case is high culpability and harm category 2, this attracts a starting point fine of £24,000.00 with a range between £8,000.00 and £90,000.00.

Some of the factors relevant to moving up or down the category range are found on page 34 of the Guideline.

Factors increasing seriousness (and hence inviting a move upwards from the starting point fine include: previous convictions (made worse if of a similar nature and are recent), motivated by financial gain, deliberately concealing the offence, a poor safety or hygiene record and, perhaps interestingly, refusal of free advice or training (a point mentioned earlier in the book in connection with the resources available to FBOs in respect of setting up food safety management systems and HACCP).

Factors reducing seriousness (and hence inviting a move downwards from the starting point) include; the absence of relevant recent convictions, steps taken to voluntarily remedy the problem, a good food safety and hygiene record, cooperation and acceptance of responsibility.

Step 3 – step back

Having applied the above factors and arrived at a fine, the court must "step back" and have regard to the objectives of sentencing in order to assess whether the fine, which has been heavily influenced by the organisation's turnover and the above factors, is "proportionate to the overall means of the offender".

Sentencing should have regard to the need for punishment, deterrence and the removal of gain obtained from the illegal activity (something different to a formal application under proceeds of crime legislation).

A long-standing feature of sentencing in food and other regulatory cases, requires that the fine has a "real economic impact" on the organisation to send a message to "both management and shareholders".

It goes without saying that senior representatives of the organisation with responsibility for food and regulatory compliance, including those at board level, should attend the sentencing hearing. This shows the court that the organisation takes the matter very seriously and the judge's sentencing remarks will be heard directly by those responsible for the organisation's activities.

The following will be relevant to assessing whether and adjustment is required:

- Profit margin – where the organisation has a high turnover but operates consistently with a small profit margin, this may lead to a downwards adjustment of the fine (the opposite will of course apply where the organisation has a high profit margin);
- Economic benefit from the offence – this might be a quantifiable sum of money gained from the non-compliance but it might include costs saved by not doing what was required or other savings;
- Putting the organisation out of business – the court will bear in mind that a high fine might result in the organisation closing with the loss of direct and indirect jobs. While the court is reluctant to

impose a fine having that effect, this may be inevitable in a particularly bad case;

There is no doubt that sections of the food sector were hit very badly by the Covid-19 pandemic. This may have led to a business which had a large turnover and a healthy profit at the time of the alleged offence having very little at the time of the court hearing. Before the court will accept a submission based on financial hardship due to the pandemic, it will need evidence showing the past and present financial situation, along with estimates for the future. It will also require evidence from the business itself about the impact on the business, how it survived, if indeed it did, and its plans for the, potentially uncertain, future.

The Guideline allows the court to impose a large fine, to reflect the seriousness of the offence, but to require it to be paid "if necessary over a number of years". This may also apply to a smaller business who has fallen on hard times due to Covid-19 or other circumstances.

Step Four – other factors

This step requires the court to have regard to the particular effect of a fine on public or charitable bodies.

If the organisation can show that the fine would have a "significant impact" on the provision of their services, the Guideline suggest that the fine should "normally be substantially reduced".

The organisation must provide some evidence of the impact, or likely impact, of a large fine. The court can consider anything that is relevant including the wider impact of a fine on the employment of staff, service users, customers and local economy.

However, the Guideline makes it clear that at step four the court is concerned with the impact of a fine on the organisation's ability to provide valuable, or sometimes essential, services. The impact of the fine on shareholders and/or directors is not to be taken into account.

Step Five – assistance to the prosecution

This step is very specific and goes well over and beyond the expected level of cooperation which is a mitigating factor at step two.

Step five applies to sections 73 and 74 of the Serious Organised Crime and Police Act 2005 and any other rule of law by which a defendant may receive a discounted sentence "in consequence of assistance given (or offered) to the prosecutor or investigator".

This is unlikely to apply in the vast majority of food law cases.

However, it may have a role to play in a particularly complex and large-scale food poisoning or misdescription case where the information assists in providing information about other participants and helps to protect consumers, thus saving the investigators a significant amount of time and resources.

Step Six – reduction for a guilty plea

As we saw earlier, fines in food cases can be very high and the reduction in sentence following a guilty plea can be quite significant. Where the guilty plea is entered at a very early stage in the legal proceedings the FBO can reasonably expect the fine to be reduced by one-third.

Where a guilty plea is entered at later stages of the proceedings the reduction may only be one-quarter and if the guilty plea is tendered at trial, there may be no reduction at all.

The Court may apply different reductions for different sets of offences as was the case in the Tesco case referred to above.

Step Seven – compensation and ancillary matters

The court will consider whether to order the defendant to pay compensation to one or more victims of the offence and it may also prohibit the defendant from being involved in the management of a food business (see below).

Step 8 – Totality principle

Where a defendant is to be sentenced for more than one offence, as is nearly always the case in food matters, the court must ensure that the overall penalty is just and proportionate (see below).

Step 9 – Reasons

When imposing its sentence, the court is required to give reasons for its decision. This is an important part of the process and can help a defendant identify whether the court may have erred in its application of the law, the facts, and the sentencing guideline, or in any other way.

Sentencing of Individuals

Before considering the effect of the Guideline, it should be recalled that individuals may also be subject to prosecution under general criminal law, as well as food law offences, as seen in:

Zaman [2017] EWCA Crim 1783 – manslaughter – allergens – imprisonment for 6 years (see the reference in chapter 5); and

Rebelo [2021] EWCA Crim 306 – manslaughter – supply of Dinitrophenol (DNP) as a food supplement for weight loss – imprisonment for 7 years

The Guideline applies to individuals and is based on the same general approach to the sentencing of organisations.

Step One – offence category

The court applies the factors to determine the offence category by reference to culpability and harm.

Culpability

The same four categories apply to the sentencing of individuals: very high, high, medium and low.

Category	Applicability
Very high	Intentional breach or flagrant disregard for the law
High	Actual foresight of, or wilful blindness to, risk of offending but risk is nevertheless taken
Medium	Offence committed through act or omission which a person exercising reasonable care would not commit.
Low	Offence committed with little fault (significant, but inadequate, efforts to address the risk; no warning indicating a risk to food safety; minor failings and an isolated incident

Harm

The categories of harm are similar to those applicable to the sentencing of organisations and similar issues arise with regard to the sentencing of individuals.

<u>Step Two – starting point and category range</u>

In order to provide the court with details of his or her finances, the defendant will be required to complete a form entitled "statement of assets and other financial circumstances". The court can require an individual to provide further information to corroborate the figures set out on the form and may require evidence of this to be given under oath.

If no information is provided or the court is not satisfied that it has been given sufficient reliable information, it may draw the inference that the defendant can pay any fine.

Having assessed the levels of culpability and harm, the court will consider whether a term of imprisonment is appropriate.

Alternatively, the court may impose a fine which is based on a percentage of the individual's relevant weekly income (see below).

The court may decide to impose a punishment between a fine and imprisonment, or it may decide not to impose a penalty.

However, where a custodial sentence is a potential outcome, the Guideline requires the court to ask itself the following questions:

1. Has the custody threshold been passed?

2. If so, is it unavoidable that a custodial sentence be imposed?

3. If so, can that sentence be suspended?

The court may also consider imposing a community penalty, the requirements of which aim to punish offenders, to change offenders' behaviour so they don't commit crime in the future, and to make amends to the victim of the crime or the local community. This might include performing a specified number of hours of unpaid work.

Where this is a potential sentence, the court must ask itself whether the community threshold has been passed and even if it has, the Guideline suggests that a fine will "normally be the most appropriate disposal".

Step two also includes a list of aggravating factors and mitigating factors, some of which mirror those applicable to the sentencing of organisations.

Additional mitigating factors relevant to individuals that might be deployed in an appropriate case include:

- Good character and/or exemplary conduct;
- Mental disorder or learning disability, where linked to the commission of the offence;

- Serious medical conditions requiring urgent, intensive or long-term treatment;

- Age and/or lack of maturity where it affects the responsibility of the offender; and

- Sole or primary care for dependent relatives.

As with all other issues relating to sentencing hearings, the court will expect to receive evidence from the defendant, and from the prosecution, before it can, or should, properly take any matters into account.

Step Three – Review the financial element of the sentence

As required by the general principles of sentencing, the court will have regard to the seriousness of the offence and the defendant's financial circumstances (see above in respect of the financial impact of Covid-19)

Step Four – Assistance to the prosecution

The court will apply the same principles as set out above as they apply to organisations.

Step Five – Reduction for Guilty Pleas

See below

Step Six – Compensation and ancillary orders

See below.

Step Seven – Totality

See below.

Step Eight – Reasons

See above.

Step Nine

The court must consider giving credit for time spent on bail.

Some points applicable to the sentencing of organisations and individuals

Compensation and ancillary orders

Compensation

The court will consider whether to award compensation to the victim of an offence who has suffered loss or damage. If it does so then the payment of compensation takes precedence over the payment of any other financial penalty where the defendant's means are limited.

Courts are generally reluctant to award compensation other than in simple and straightforward cases where the amount can easily and readily be ascertained. While this was, and has been, the generally accepted approach, courts more willing to entertain applications for compensation in a broader spectrum of cases, for example where the victim's only realistic chance of receiving compensation was through the criminal courts, there was no recompense by virtue of an insurance policy and/or if there was an ineffective remedy in civil proceedings.

In a food case the court may be willing to entertain a claim for compensation in a food poisoning claim and if so, the judge might refer to the Judicial Studies Board's "Guidelines for the Assessment of General Damages in Personal Injury Cases".

Hygiene Prohibition Order (HPO)

Following conviction for an offence the Food Safety and Hygiene (England) Regulations 2013, and its Welsh equivalent, the court may "impose a prohibition on the food business operator participating in the management of any food business".

The Regulations specify that the court may impose such a hygiene prohibition order where it thinks it is "proper to do so in all the circumstances of the case.

This may be because of the general poor hygiene record and/or a history of failing to heed warnings or advice and/or the court has little confidence that the defendant will comply fully with legal obligations in the future. Furthermore, the court will have regard to the deterrent effect of a HPO to send a powerful message to others working in the food industry that they must comply strictly with the requirements of rigorous food hygiene.

An HPO may be made against an individual and a corporate defendant.

Director's disqualification

Where a person is convicted of an indictable offence in connection with the promotion, formation, management of a company, and other specified company related activities, (which includes all food offences of that description whether or not they are within the ambit of the Sentencing Guideline), the court may order that the person may not be a director of a company or whether directly or indirectly be involved in the management of a company.

Such an order is there to protect the public from people who, for reasons of dishonesty, or naivety or incompetence, abuse their role and status as director. The period of disqualification is up to 15 years when the person is sentenced in the crown court (the maximum is 5 years in the magistrates' court).

Totality principle

Where a court is sentencing a defendant in respect of more than one offence the court determines the sentence for each offence and then assesses whether the total sentence is just and proportionate.

If, having regard to all matters the court thinks that it is then the aggregate sentence remains.

If not, the court has a number of options to arrive at a just and proportionate aggregate sentence:

1. For offences committed on the same occasion, the court may impose a fine for one offence (usually the most serious offence) and

then in respect of the other offences, reduce what would otherwise be the sentence for other offences or impose no separate penalty;

2. For offences committed on more than one occasion, the court may consider imposing a mixture of consecutive and concurrent sentences.

Prosecution costs

The defendant will be required to pay the costs of the prosecution to the extent that they are "just and reasonable" – section 18 of the Prosecution of Offenders Act 1985. The prosecution should produce a breakdown of its costs and this should be made available to the defendant at the sentencing hearing, if not beforehand.

The court does not tend to determine costs in the same detailed manner as might be found in a civil case, but the court may require an explanation of how the costs have been incurred by the prosecution (including legal, investigative and experts' fees).

Having been supplied with the prosecution's costs breakdown, it is commonplace for there to be an agreement between the parties as to the amount of costs that the defendant agrees to pay.

In a complex case, even following a guilty plea, the prosecution's costs can be high, possibly in the tens of thousands of pounds, and so the defendant should carefully review the costs schedule and, where appropriate, make submissions to the court on those aspects which the FBO does not believe are "just and reasonable".

Pragmatism has a part to play because if the court needs to consider costs in detail this may require an additional hearing and the costs of that might outweigh the potential saving for the defendant.

Victim surcharge

When the court imposes a sentence, it must also make provision for the payment of the appropriate victim surcharge which is used to fund victim support services (see section 42 Sentencing Act 2020 and the Regulations which set the amount of the surcharge).

Time to pay

Once the court has made a final determination on the payment of fines, compensation (if any) and costs, it will make an order for the payment of the total amount. The court may require the amount to be paid immediately or it may allow a period of time (for example 28 days) in which the total sum must be paid.

If, after the hearing, the defendant gets into difficulty in paying the financial penalty contact should be made with the court office otherwise the court might take steps to enforce payment.

Proceeds of crime

In an appropriate case the defendant might face an application under the proceeds of crime legislation to remove financial gain achieved through criminality.

Conclusion

Sentencing of food cases is now subject to the step-by-step approach envisaged by the Guideline although, in order to reach a just and proportionate sentence, the Guideline should not be followed rigidly.

However, it is crucial that all parties have regard to those pieces of evidence that have particular relevance to the court's determination of the appropriate sentence. The prosecution and defence should produce written submissions setting out their respective positions, in advance of the hearing.

This may involve them collaborating or setting out where they agree and disagree in an attempt to assist the court and save time and resources (in this regard see the observations at paragraph 51 in the case of *R (Health and Safety Executive) v ATE Truck & Trailer Sales Ltd* [2018] [2018] EWCA Crim 752.

Where agreement cannot be reached, the court will decide if it can properly sentence the defendant based on the written material or whether evidence needs to be heard.

Criticisms have been made of the Sentencing Guideline in that it does not adequately with organisations with very large turnovers. It is not known whether another category will need to be inserted to reflect a turnover in excess of £50 million. If another category is inserted into the Guideline, what level of turnover should be chosen and how will this be reflected in the starting point and range of financial penalties.

CHAPTER ELEVEN

CONCLUSIONS AND THE FUTURE FOR FOOD LAW IN THE UK

Food law is made up of so many laws, regulations and policies that this book can only hope to scratch the surface of such a vast topic. There are matters that I could, and perhaps should, have included, but it was necessary be selective in order for the book to be a readable and reasonably short practical guide.

The last few months have created much change, concern, anguish, administration, bureaucracy and uncertainty for many food businesses and consumers. Unfortunately, this is likely to continue while all stakeholders get used to the new approach.

Implementation Period (IP) completion day, 11 pm 31 December 2020 was undoubtedly a significant event.

As a consequence of the UK's departure from the UK, it has been necessary to impose border controls on imports coming into GB from the EU. How this is achieved and when the changes took and will take effect are set out in a useful document called "The Border with the European Union Importing and Exporting Goods" (the Border Operating Model). Due to Covid-19 some dates have been put back from late 2021 into 2022.

Other changes concerning the regulation of foodstuffs in GB will take effect over the coming months.

Great Britain now has the power to "go it alone" in terms of food law and policy but it may need to have regard to broader food-related priorities such as nutrition and healthy eating, climate change, food waste, sustainability and security.

It must also be cognisant of what changes are taking place in the EU and both the UK and the EU should seek to avoid laws and policies that create a divergence in regulatory approach. If the changes are too significant it may be harder to enter or remain in those other markets and this may result in businesses having to seek new trading opportunities.

This could also have an impact on important policy issues such as animal welfare, obesity and healthy eating, trying to reduce the carbon footprint of goods and people and which could have an adverse impact on climate change goals and other longer-term strategies.

Nevertheless, GB has enacted domestic legislation as part of its aim to benefit its citizens and push forward certain policy agendas, particularly around targeting obesity.

As mentioned already, 1 October 2021 saw the introduction of Natasha's law as an amendment to the Food Information Regulations which requires allergy labelling for foods prepacked for direct sale (PPDS) (see chapter 5).

On 6 April 2022, the Calorie Labelling (Out of Home Sector) (England) Regulations 2021 will come into force. The out of home sector (restaurants, fast-food outlets, pubs etc.) typically sells non-prepacked food which does not require nutritional information.

The regulations apply to larger businesses (more than 250 employees) and will require calories to be labelled next to items on paper and online menus.

They are part of the obesity reduction strategy and as consumers are used to seeing calorie labelling on pre-packed food it is hoped that the new regulations will bring that familiarity to non-prepacked foods and help consumers make healthier decisions. The effectiveness of the plan may depend on how well consumers can be informed and educated about calories and their role in a healthy and balanced diet.

Requiring calorie labelling on non-prepacked foods may encourage businesses to reformulate the food and drink they offer and provide lower calorie options for their customers.

Although currently only in draft form, the Food (Promotion and Placement) (England) Regulations 2021 are intended to come into force on 1 October 2022 (and not April 2022 as originally planned).

The regulations are another part of the strategy to reduce childhood obesity and they will apply restrictions in respect of the volume price and location in store (or online) of "specified food" defined as food which:

(a) is schedule 1 food;

(b) is less healthy (as defined); and

(c) is not food to which the charity food sales provision

As with the calories regulations mentioned above, these regulations, assuming they become law, need to be considered in detail to see what is, and what is not, in scope and how businesses will be expected to comply with them

For present purposes it may suffice to identify some of the food items listed by category in schedule 1:

- Soft drinks with added sugar
- Crisps, pretzels and salted popcorn (but not raw, roasted, coated or flavoured nuts)
- Chocolate and sweets
- Cakes and cupcakes
- Pizza
- Danish pastries

Whether any, or all of the new regulations will achieve their goals remains to be seen.

It also raises the age-old debate about how best to achieve these aims; by legislating, by education, by science, by promoting healthy eating and encouraging activity and exercise, and/or by applying the test of 'all things in moderation'.

While it is impossible to know what *will* happen next, an indication of what *might* happen can be seen from the National Food Strategy, Part 2, which was published in July 2021.

The strategy focuses on England but contains information related to and relevant to Wales, Scotland and Northern Ireland.

A glance at the Executive Summary quickly sets the scene; "The food system we have today is both a miracle and a disaster", "the food we eat – and the way we produce it – is doing terrible damage to our planet and to our health." The message could not be clearer; "The UK now has a once-in-a-lifetime opportunity to reshape the food system."

The Strategy makes 14, some of which are arguably quite radical, recommendations, grouped under the following four headings, to meet its strategic objectives:

1. To escape the junk food cycle to protect the NHS;

2. To reduce diet-related inequality;

3. To make the best use of our land; and

4. To create a long-term shift in our food culture

The Plan is ambitious but it might be felt that it needs to be if real change is to follow.

Finally, a word about the Environment Act 2021 which passed into law in early November 2021. There are likely to be some shared policy areas with the food industry around matters such as single-use plastics, waste and recycling.

The Environmental Protection (Plastic Straws, Cotton Buds and Stirrers) (England) Regulations 2020 which created offences by a person who in the course of a business:

- supplies or offers to supply to an end user a single-use plastic straw, other than an attached plastic straw; or
- supplies or offers to supply to an end user a drink product with an attached plastic straw

There are many other strategies, policies and legislation in the pipeline which will affect food business operators and consumers in the UK and within the four nations of the UK.

Irrespective of, or perhaps because of, the many challenges facing the food industry, competent authorities and consumers, food law is, and will continue to be, a fascinating, and relevant, subject from so many different perspectives.

MORE BOOKS BY LAW BRIEF PUBLISHING

A selection of our other titles available now:-

'A Practical Guide to Transgender Law' by Robin Moira White & Nicola Newbegin
'Artificial Intelligence – The Practical Legal Issues (2nd Edition)' by John Buyers
'A Practical Guide to Challenging Sham Marriage Allegations in Immigration Law' by Priya Solanki
'A Practical Guide to New Build Conveyancing' by Paul Sams & Rebecca East
'A Practical Guide to Inherited Wealth on Divorce' by Hayley Trim
'A Practical Guide to Shareholder Disputes in Family Businesses' by Ed Weeks
'A Practical Guide to the Law of Forests in Scotland' by Philip Buchan
'A Practical Guide to Health and Medical Cases in Immigration Law' by Rebecca Chapman & Miranda Butler
'A Practical Guide to Bad Character Evidence for Criminal Practitioners by Aparna Rao
'A Practical Guide to Environmental Enforcement' by Christopher Badger & Stuart Jessop
'A Practical Guide to Hoarding and Mental Health for Housing Lawyers' by Rachel Coyle
'A Practical Guide to Psychiatric Claims in Personal Injury – 2nd Edition' by Liam Ryan
'Stephens on Contractual Indemnities' by Richard Stephens
'A Practical Guide to the EU Succession Regulation' by Richard Frimston
'A Practical Guide to Solicitor and Client Costs – 2nd Edition' by Robin Dunne
'Constructive Dismissal – Practice Pointers and Principles' by Benjimin Burgher
'A Practical Guide to Religion and Belief Discrimination Claims in the Workplace' by Kashif Ali
'A Practical Guide to the Law of Medical Treatment Decisions' by Ben Troke

‘Fundamental Dishonesty and QOCS in Personal Injury Proceedings: Law and Practice’ by Jake Rowley

‘A Practical Guide to the Law in Relation to School Exclusions’ by Charlotte Hadfield & Alice de Coverley

‘A Practical Guide to Divorce for the Silver Separators’ by Karin Walker

‘The Right to be Forgotten – The Law and Practical Issues’ by Melissa Stock

‘A Practical Guide to Planning Law and Rights of Way in National Parks, the Broads and AONBs’ by James Maurici QC, James Neill et al

‘A Practical Guide to Election Law’ by Tom Tabori

‘A Practical Guide to the Law in Relation to Surrogacy’ by Andrew Powell

‘A Practical Guide to Claims Arising from Fatal Accidents – 2nd Edition’ by James Patience

‘A Practical Guide to the Ownership of Employee Inventions – From Entitlement to Compensation’ by James Tumbridge & Ashley Roughton

‘A Practical Guide to Asbestos Claims’ by Jonathan Owen & Gareth McAloon

‘A Practical Guide to Stamp Duty Land Tax in England and Northern Ireland’ by Suzanne O’Hara

‘A Practical Guide to the Law of Farming Partnerships’ by Philip Whitcomb

‘Covid-19, Homeworking and the Law – The Essential Guide to Employment and GDPR Issues’ by Forbes Solicitors

‘Covid-19, Force Majeure and Frustration of Contracts – The Essential Guide’ by Keith Markham

‘Covid-19 and Criminal Law – The Essential Guide’ by Ramya Nagesh

‘Covid-19 and Family Law in England and Wales – The Essential Guide’ by Safda Mahmood

‘A Practical Guide to the Law of Unlawful Eviction and Harassment – 2nd Edition’ by Stephanie Lovegrove

‘Covid-19, Residential Property, Equity Release and Enfranchisement – The Essential Guide’ by Paul Sams and Louise Uphill

‘Covid-19, Brexit and the Law of Commercial Leases – The Essential Guide’ by Mark Shelton

‘A Practical Guide to Costs in Personal Injury Claims – 2nd Edition’ by Matthew Hoe

'A Practical Guide to the General Data Protection Regulation (GDPR) – 2nd Edition' by Keith Markham
'Ellis on Credit Hire – Sixth Edition' by Aidan Ellis & Tim Kevan
'A Practical Guide to Working with Litigants in Person and McKenzie Friends in Family Cases' by Stuart Barlow
'Protecting Unregistered Brands: A Practical Guide to the Law of Passing Off' by Lorna Brazell
'A Practical Guide to Secondary Liability and Joint Enterprise Post-Jogee' by Joanne Cecil & James Mehigan
'A Practical Guide to the Pre-Action RTA Claims Protocol for Personal Injury Lawyers' by Antonia Ford
'A Practical Guide to Neighbour Disputes and the Law' by Alexander Walsh
'A Practical Guide to Forfeiture of Leases' by Mark Shelton
'A Practical Guide to Coercive Control for Legal Practitioners and Victims' by Rachel Horman
'A Practical Guide to Rights Over Airspace and Subsoil' by Daniel Gatty
'Tackling Disclosure in the Criminal Courts – A Practitioner's Guide' by Narita Bahra QC & Don Ramble
'A Practical Guide to the Law of Driverless Cars – Second Edition' by Alex Glassbrook, Emma Northey & Scarlett Milligan
'A Practical Guide to TOLATA Claims' by Greg Williams
'A Practical Guide to Elderly Law – 2nd Edition' by Justin Patten
'A Practical Guide to the Law of Prescription in Scotland' by Andrew Foyle
'A Practical Guide to the Construction and Rectification of Wills and Trust Instruments' by Edward Hewitt
'A Practical Guide to the Law of Bullying and Harassment in the Workplace' by Philip Hyland
'How to Be a Freelance Solicitor: A Practical Guide to the SRA-Regulated Freelance Solicitor Model' by Paul Bennett
'A Practical Guide to Prison Injury Claims' by Malcolm Johnson
'A Practical Guide to the Small Claims Track - 2nd Edition' by Dominic Bright
'A Practical Guide to Advising Clients at the Police Station' by Colin Stephen McKeown-Beaumont

'A Practical Guide to Antisocial Behaviour Injunctions' by Iain Wightwick
'Practical Mediation: A Guide for Mediators, Advocates, Advisers, Lawyers, and Students in Civil, Commercial, Business, Property, Workplace, and Employment Cases' by Jonathan Dingle with John Sephton
'The Mini-Pupillage Workbook' by David Boyle
'A Practical Guide to Crofting Law' by Brian Inkster
'A Practical Guide to Spousal Maintenance' by Liz Cowell
'A Practical Guide to the Law of Domain Names and Cybersquatting' by Andrew Clemson
'A Practical Guide to the Law of Gender Pay Gap Reporting' by Harini Iyengar
'A Practical Guide to the Rights of Grandparents in Children Proceedings' by Stuart Barlow
'NHS Whistleblowing and the Law' by Joseph England
'Employment Law and the Gig Economy' by Nigel Mackay & Annie Powell
'A Practical Guide to Noise Induced Hearing Loss (NIHL) Claims' by Andrew Mckie, Ian Skeate, Gareth McAloon
'An Introduction to Beauty Negligence Claims – A Practical Guide for the Personal Injury Practitioner' by Greg Almond
'Intercompany Agreements for Transfer Pricing Compliance' by Paul Sutton
'Zen and the Art of Mediation' by Martin Plowman
'A Practical Guide to the SRA Principles, Individual and Law Firm Codes of Conduct 2019 – What Every Law Firm Needs to Know' by Paul Bennett
'A Practical Guide to Adoption for Family Lawyers' by Graham Pegg
'A Practical Guide to Industrial Disease Claims' by Andrew Mckie & Ian Skeate
'A Practical Guide to Redundancy' by Philip Hyland
'A Practical Guide to Vicarious Liability' by Mariel Irvine
'A Practical Guide to Applications for Landlord's Consent and Variation of Leases' by Mark Shelton
'A Practical Guide to Relief from Sanctions Post-Mitchell and Denton' by Peter Causton
'A Practical Guide to Equity Release for Advisors' by Paul Sams
'A Practical Guide to Financial Services Claims' by Chris Hegarty

'The Law of Houses in Multiple Occupation: A Practical Guide to HMO Proceedings' by Julian Hunt
'Occupiers, Highways and Defective Premises Claims: A Practical Guide Post-Jackson – 2nd Edition' by Andrew Mckie
'A Practical Guide to Financial Ombudsman Service Claims' by Adam Temple & Robert Scrivenor
'A Practical Guide to Advising Schools on Employment Law' by Jonathan Holden
'A Practical Guide to Running Housing Disrepair and Cavity Wall Claims: 2nd Edition' by Andrew Mckie & Ian Skeate
'A Practical Guide to Holiday Sickness Claims – 2nd Edition' by Andrew Mckie & Ian Skeate
'Arguments and Tactics for Personal Injury and Clinical Negligence Claims' by Dorian Williams
'A Practical Guide to Drone Law' by Rufus Ballaster, Andrew Firman, Eleanor Clot
'A Practical Guide to Compliance for Personal Injury Firms Working With Claims Management Companies' by Paul Bennett
'RTA Allegations of Fraud in a Post-Jackson Era: The Handbook – 2nd Edition' by Andrew Mckie
'RTA Personal Injury Claims: A Practical Guide Post-Jackson' by Andrew Mckie
'On Experts: CPR35 for Lawyers and Experts' by David Boyle
'An Introduction to Personal Injury Law' by David Boyle
'A Practical Guide to Subtle Brain Injury Claims' by Pankaj Madan

www.ingramcontent.com/pod-product-compliance
Lightning Source LLC
LaVergne TN
LVHW022043200926
848481LV00003B/767